GETTYSBURG

THE GRAPHIC NOVEL

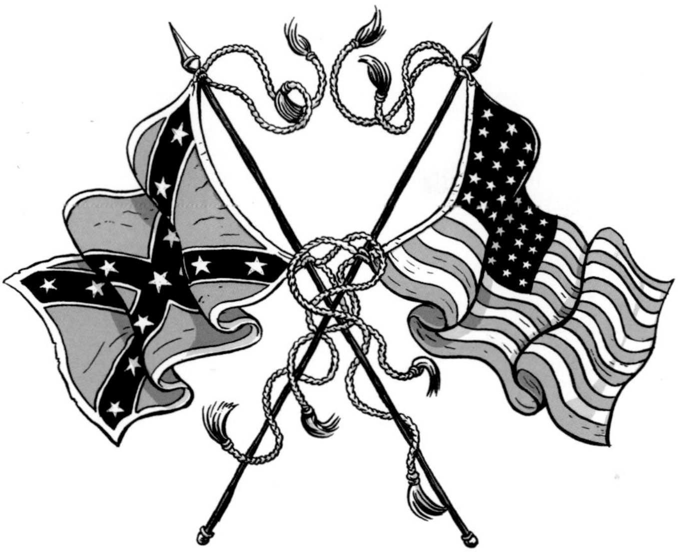

WRITTEN AND ILLUSTRATED BY

C. M. BUTZER

THE BOWEN PRESS
Collins
AN IMPRINT OF HARPERCOLLINSPUBLISHERS

Collins is an imprint of HarperCollins Publishers.

Gettysburg: The Graphic Novel

Copyright © 2009 by C. M. Butzer

Manufactured in China.

HarperCollins Children's Books, a division of HarperCollins Publishers,

1350 Avenue of the Americas, New York, NY 10019.

www.harpercollinschildrens.com

Library of Congress Cataloging-in-Publication Data

Butzer, C. M.

Gettysburg : the graphic novel / written and illustrated by C. M. Butzer. — 1st ed. p. cm.

ISBN 978-0-06-156176-4 (trade bdg.) — ISBN 978-0-06-156175-7 (pbk bdg.)

1. Gettysburg, Battle of, Gettysburg, Pa., 1863—Juvenile literature. 2. Lincoln,

Abraham, 1809–1865. Gettysburg address—Juvenile literature. I. Title.

E475.53.B985 2009   2008010657   973.7'349—dc22   CIP   AC

2 4 6 8 10 9 7 5 3 1

❖

First Edition

To my parents, my brother, Scott, and to Margary.

Without their endless support and encouragement,

making comics would be near impossible.

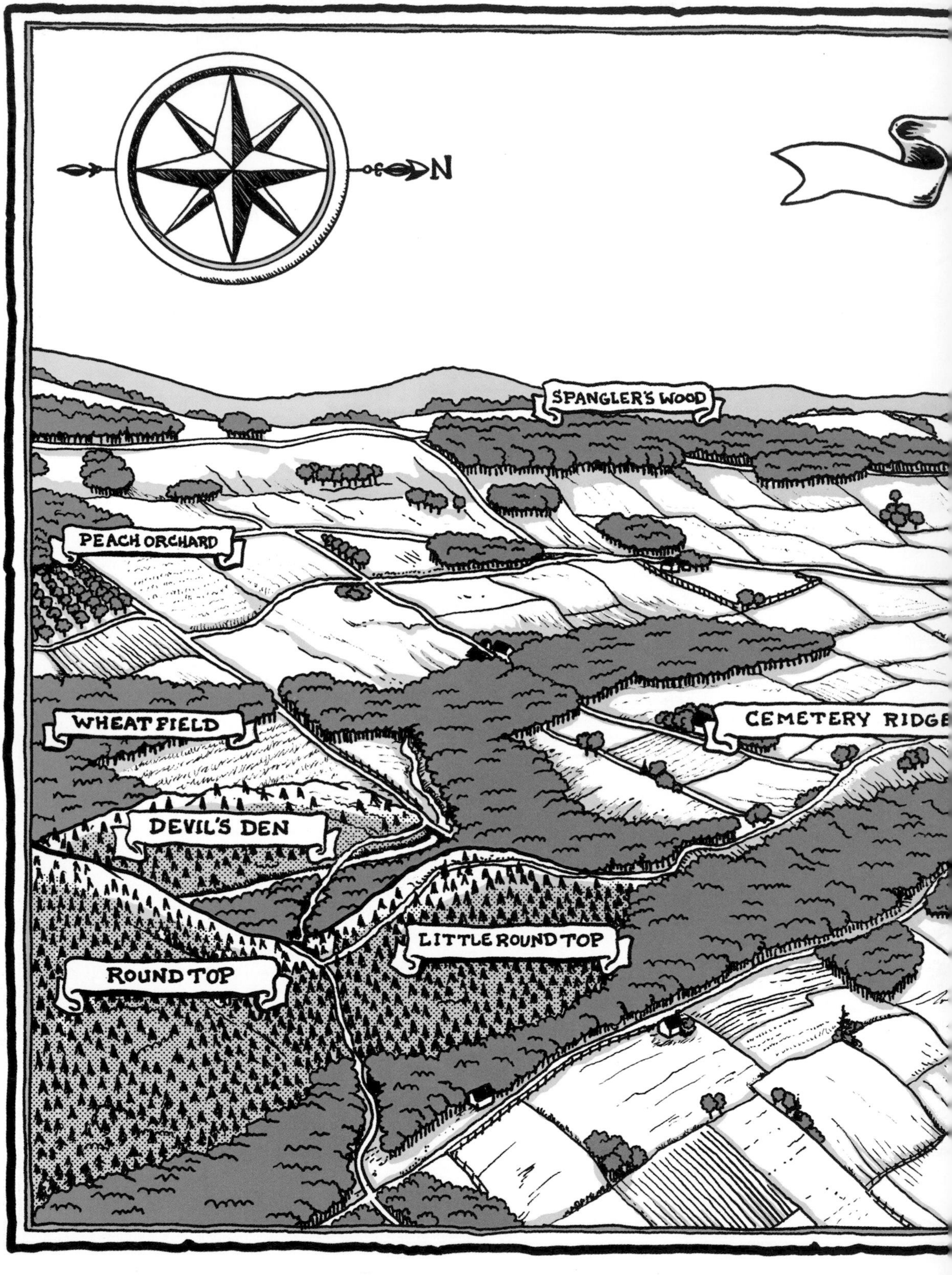
N
SPANGLER'S WOOD
PEACH ORCHARD
WHEATFIELD
CEMETERY RIDGE
DEVIL'S DEN
LITTLE ROUND TOP
ROUND TOP

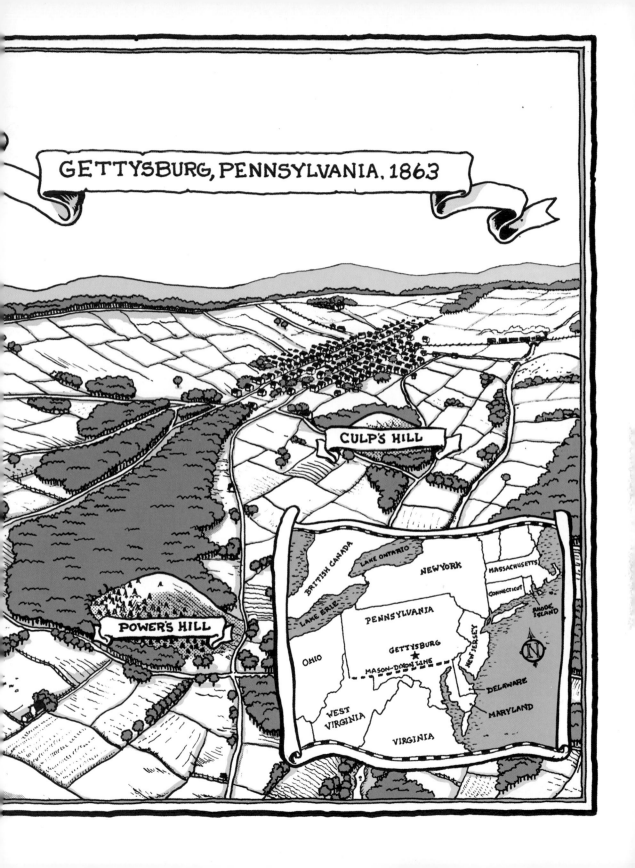

GETTYSBURG, PENNSYLVANIA, 1863

CULP'S HILL

POWER'S HILL

BRITISH CANADA

LAKE ONTARIO

NEW YORK

MASSACHUSETTS

CONNECTICUT

LAKE ERIE

PENNSYLVANIA

RHODE ISLAND

OHIO

GETTYSBURG

NEW JERSEY

MASON-DIXON LINE

DELAWARE

WEST VIRGINIA

MARYLAND

VIRGINIA

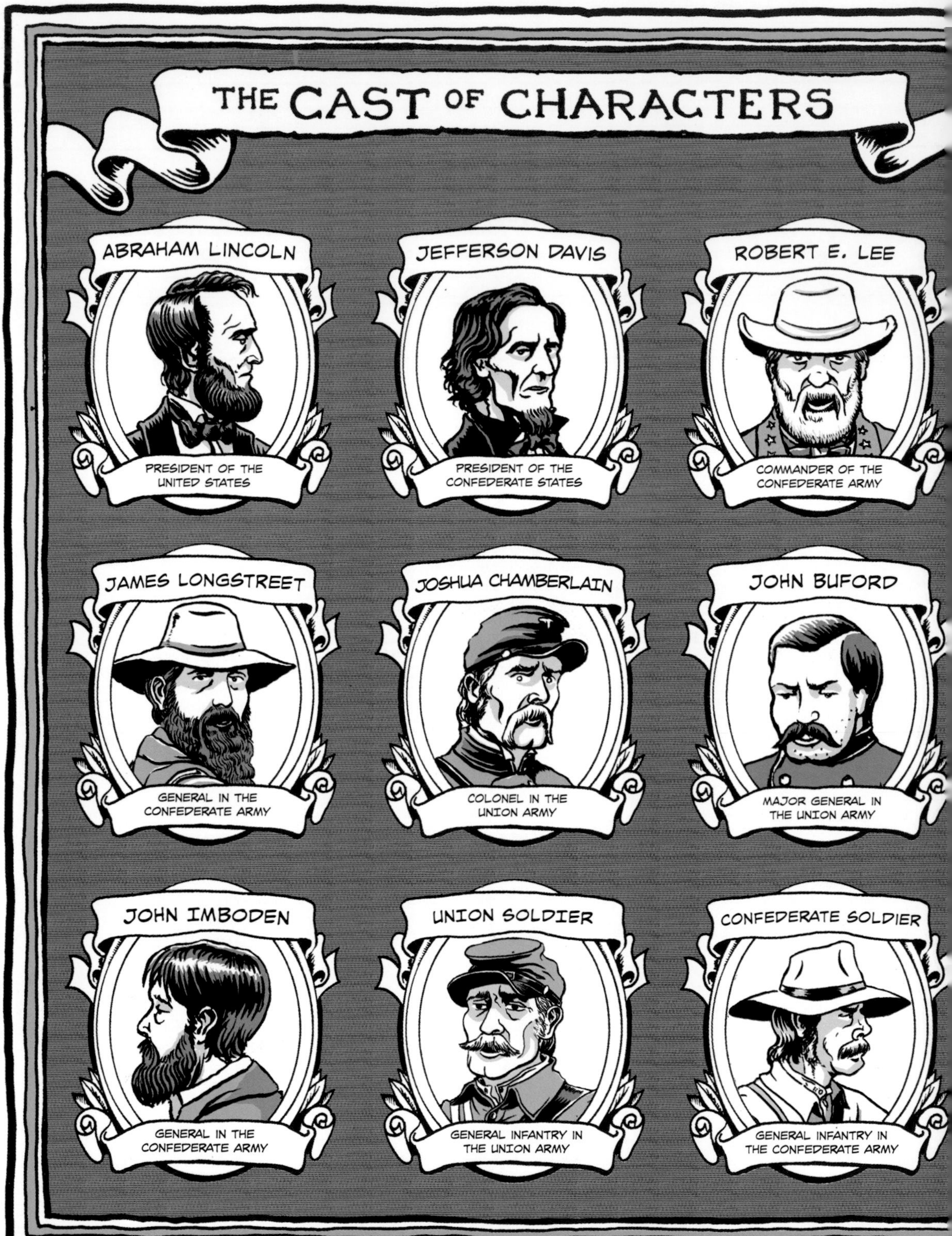
THE CAST OF CHARACTERS
ABRAHAM LINCOLN
PRESIDENT OF THE UNITED STATES
JEFFERSON DAVIS
PRESIDENT OF THE CONFEDERATE STATES
ROBERT E. LEE
COMMANDER OF THE CONFEDERATE ARMY
JAMES LONGSTREET
GENERAL IN THE CONFEDERATE ARMY
JOSHUA CHAMBERLAIN
COLONEL IN THE UNION ARMY
JOHN BUFORD
MAJOR GENERAL IN THE UNION ARMY
JOHN IMBODEN
GENERAL IN THE CONFEDERATE ARMY
UNION SOLDIER
GENERAL INFANTRY IN THE UNION ARMY
CONFEDERATE SOLDIER
GENERAL INFANTRY IN THE CONFEDERATE ARMY

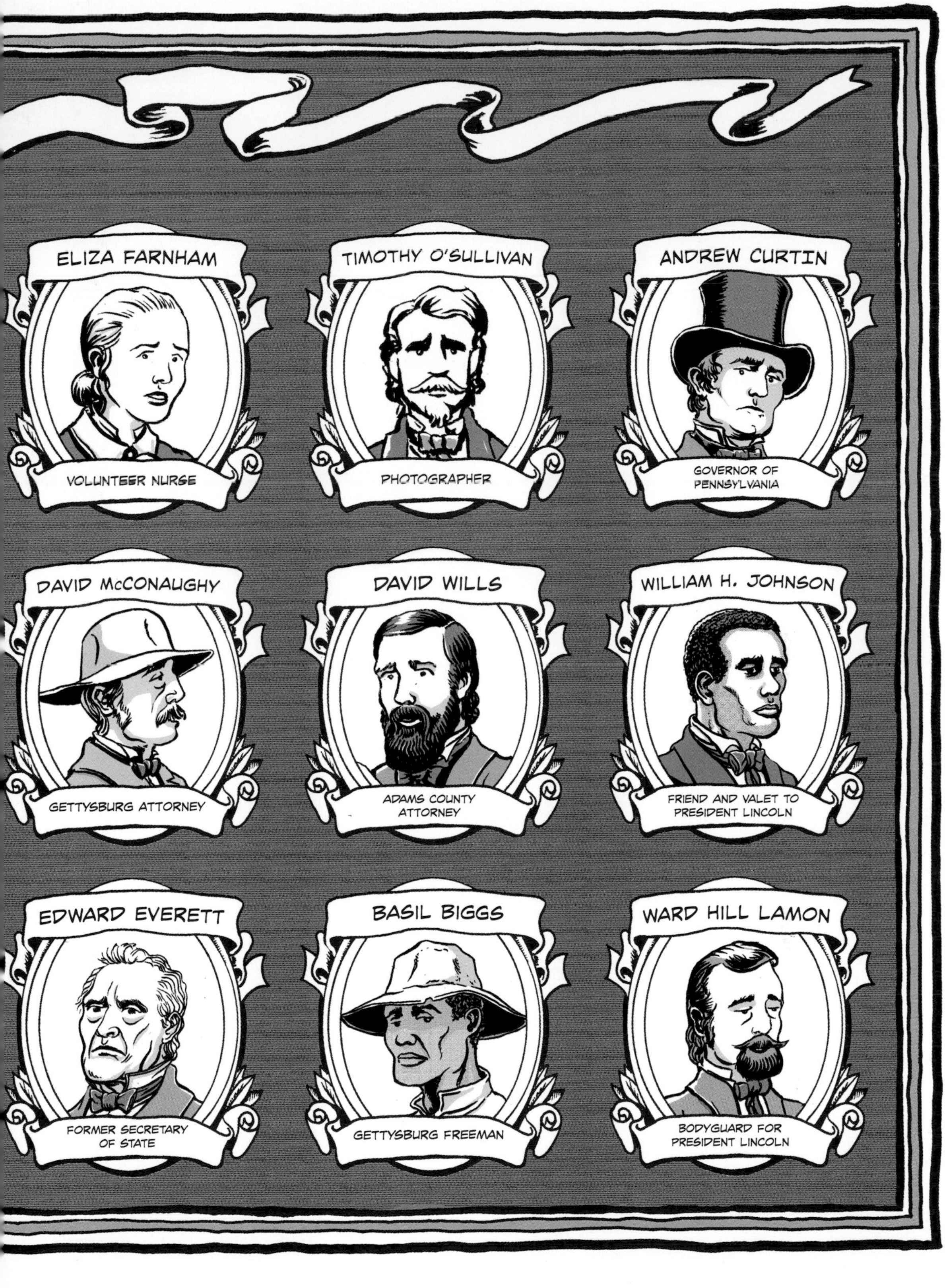
ELIZA FARNHAM
VOLUNTEER NURSE
TIMOTHY O'SULLIVAN
PHOTOGRAPHER
ANDREW CURTIN
GOVERNOR OF PENNSYLVANIA
DAVID McCONAUGHY
GETTYSBURG ATTORNEY
DAVID WILLS
ADAMS COUNTY ATTORNEY
WILLIAM H. JOHNSON
FRIEND AND VALET TO PRESIDENT LINCOLN
EDWARD EVERETT
FORMER SECRETARY OF STATE
BASIL BIGGS
GETTYSBURG FREEMAN
WARD HILL LAMON
BODYGUARD FOR PRESIDENT LINCOLN

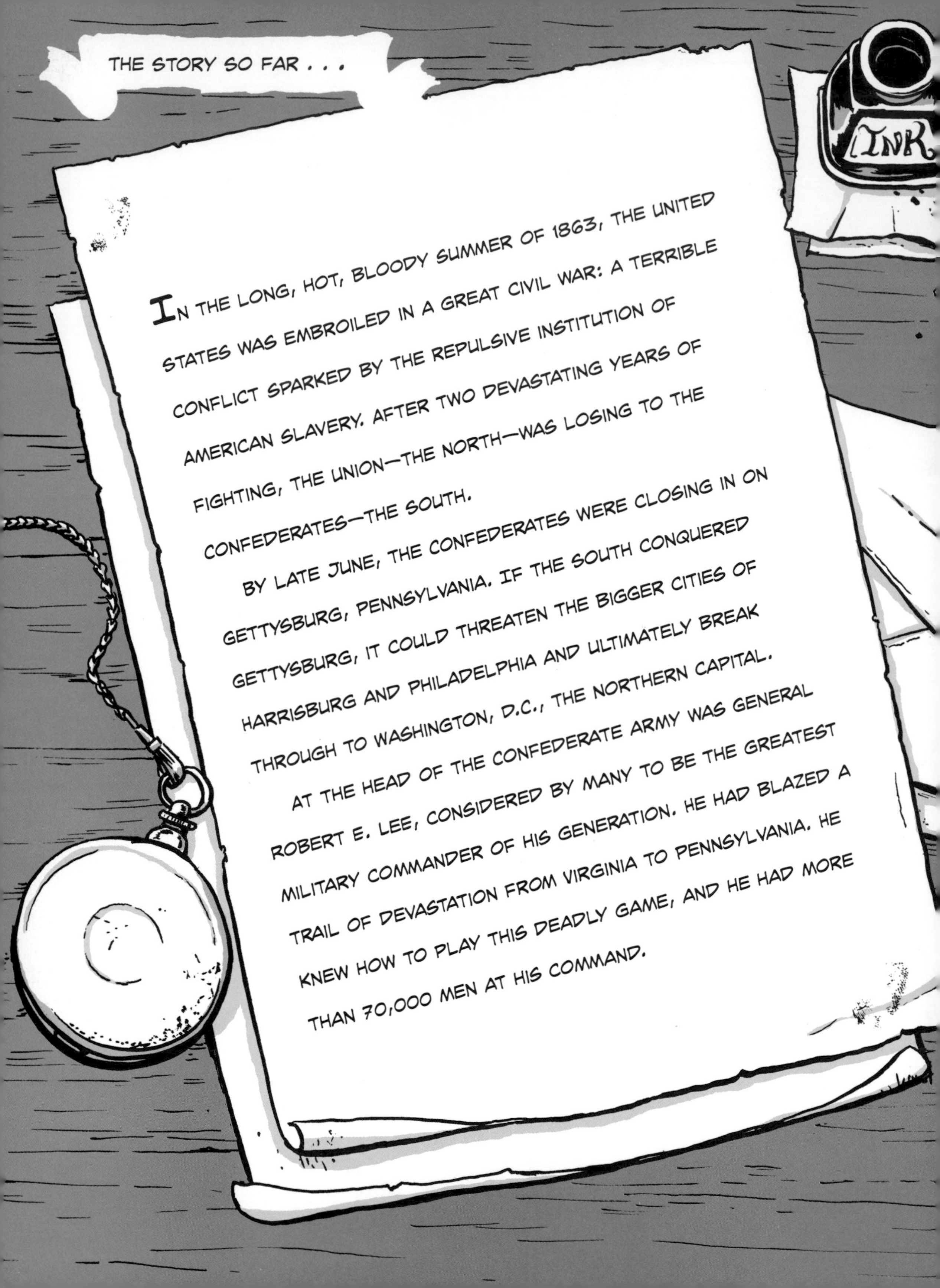
THE STORY SO FAR . . .
IN THE LONG, HOT, BLOODY SUMMER OF 1863, THE UNITED STATES WAS EMBROILED IN A GREAT CIVIL WAR: A TERRIBLE CONFLICT SPARKED BY THE REPULSIVE INSTITUTION OF AMERICAN SLAVERY. AFTER TWO DEVASTATING YEARS OF FIGHTING, THE UNION—THE NORTH—WAS LOSING TO THE CONFEDERATES—THE SOUTH.
BY LATE JUNE, THE CONFEDERATES WERE CLOSING IN ON GETTYSBURG, PENNSYLVANIA. IF THE SOUTH CONQUERED GETTYSBURG, IT COULD THREATEN THE BIGGER CITIES OF HARRISBURG AND PHILADELPHIA AND ULTIMATELY BREAK THROUGH TO WASHINGTON, D.C., THE NORTHERN CAPITAL.
AT THE HEAD OF THE CONFEDERATE ARMY WAS GENERAL ROBERT E. LEE, CONSIDERED BY MANY TO BE THE GREATEST MILITARY COMMANDER OF HIS GENERATION. HE HAD BLAZED A TRAIL OF DEVASTATION FROM VIRGINIA TO PENNSYLVANIA. HE KNEW HOW TO PLAY THIS DEADLY GAME, AND HE HAD MORE THAN 70,000 MEN AT HIS COMMAND.
INK

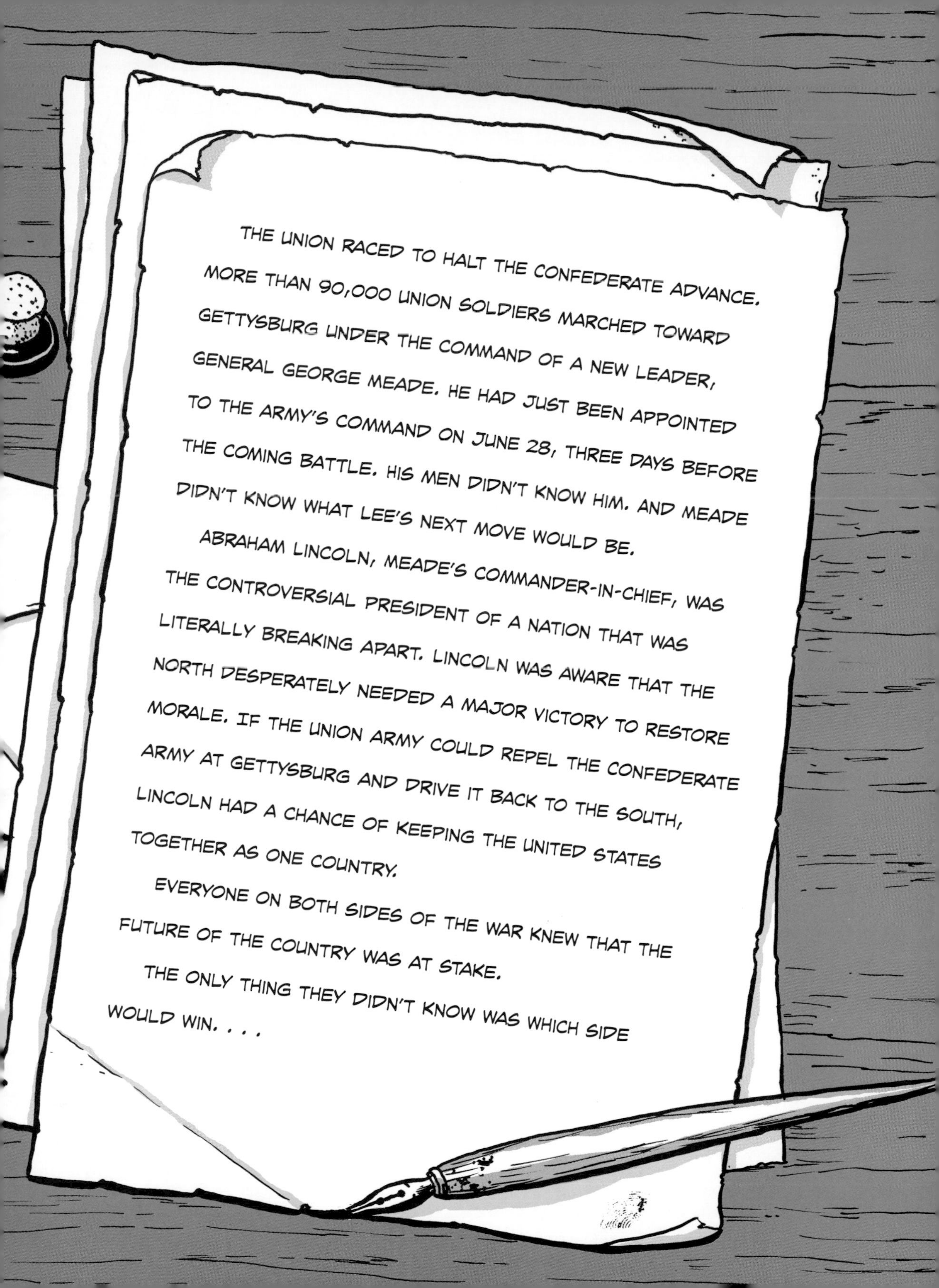
THE UNION RACED TO HALT THE CONFEDERATE ADVANCE. MORE THAN 90,000 UNION SOLDIERS MARCHED TOWARD GETTYSBURG UNDER THE COMMAND OF A NEW LEADER, GENERAL GEORGE MEADE. HE HAD JUST BEEN APPOINTED TO THE ARMY'S COMMAND ON JUNE 28, THREE DAYS BEFORE THE COMING BATTLE. HIS MEN DIDN'T KNOW HIM. AND MEADE DIDN'T KNOW WHAT LEE'S NEXT MOVE WOULD BE.
ABRAHAM LINCOLN, MEADE'S COMMANDER-IN-CHIEF, WAS THE CONTROVERSIAL PRESIDENT OF A NATION THAT WAS LITERALLY BREAKING APART. LINCOLN WAS AWARE THAT THE NORTH DESPERATELY NEEDED A MAJOR VICTORY TO RESTORE MORALE. IF THE UNION ARMY COULD REPEL THE CONFEDERATE ARMY AT GETTYSBURG AND DRIVE IT BACK TO THE SOUTH, LINCOLN HAD A CHANCE OF KEEPING THE UNITED STATES TOGETHER AS ONE COUNTRY.
EVERYONE ON BOTH SIDES OF THE WAR KNEW THAT THE FUTURE OF THE COUNTRY WAS AT STAKE.
THE ONLY THING THEY DIDN'T KNOW WAS WHICH SIDE WOULD WIN. . . .

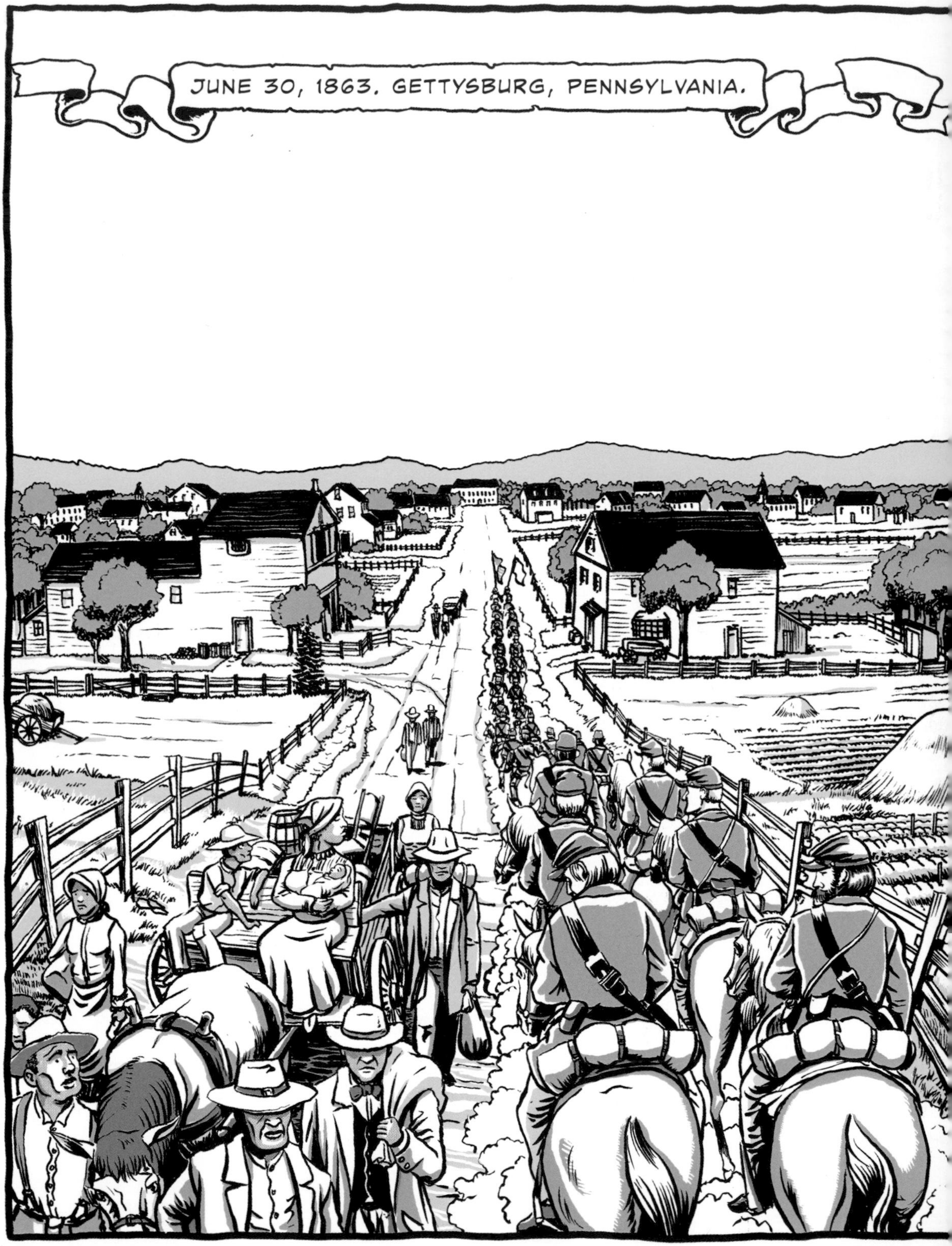
JUNE 30, 1863. GETTYSBURG, PENNSYLVANIA.

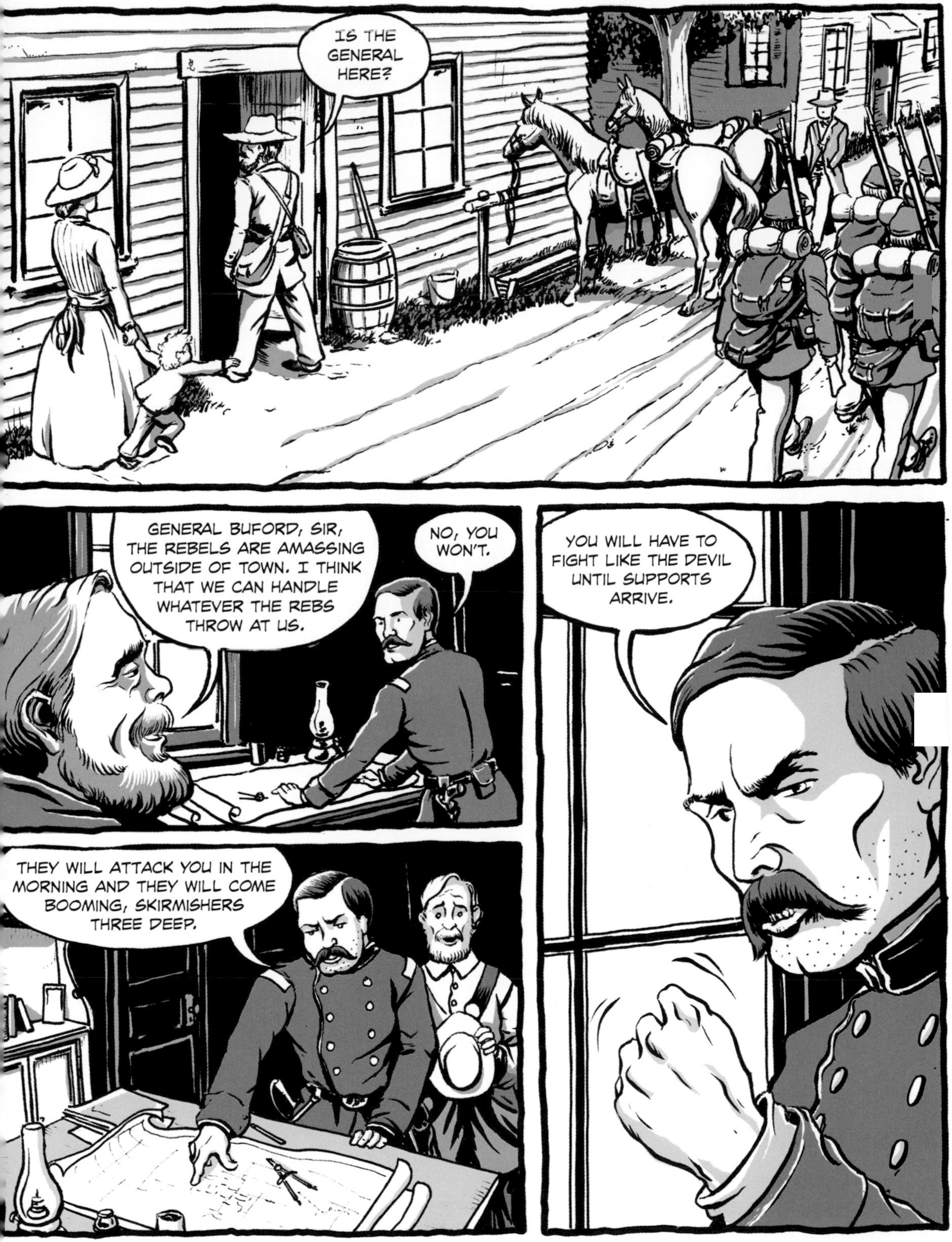
IS THE GENERAL HERE?
GENERAL BUFORD, SIR, THE REBELS ARE AMASSING OUTSIDE OF TOWN. I THINK THAT WE CAN HANDLE WHATEVER THE REBS THROW AT US.
NO, YOU WON'T.
THEY WILL ATTACK YOU IN THE MORNING AND THEY WILL COME BOOMING, SKIRMISHERS THREE DEEP.
YOU WILL HAVE TO FIGHT LIKE THE DEVIL UNTIL SUPPORTS ARRIVE.

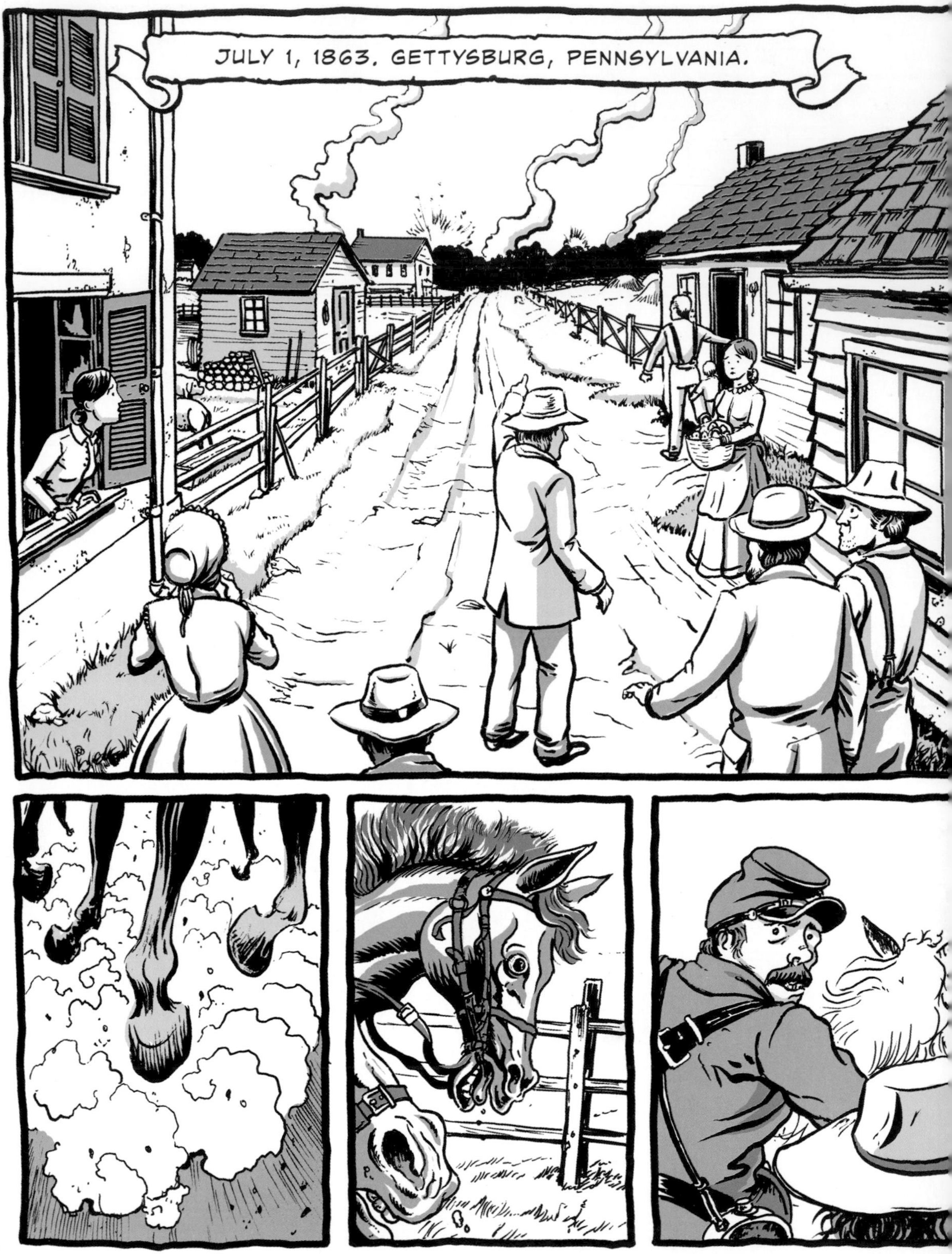
JULY 1, 1863. GETTYSBURG, PENNSYLVANIA.

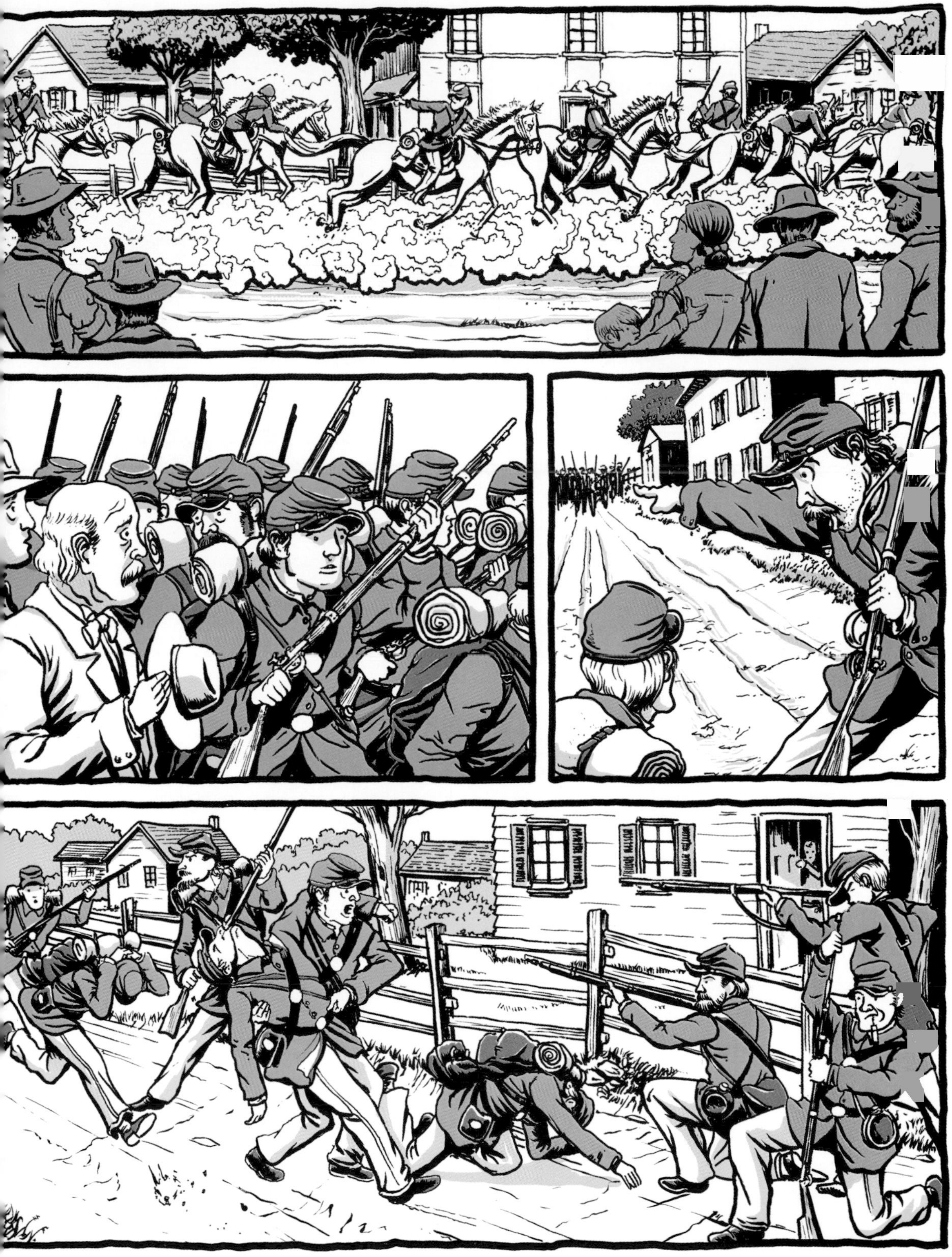

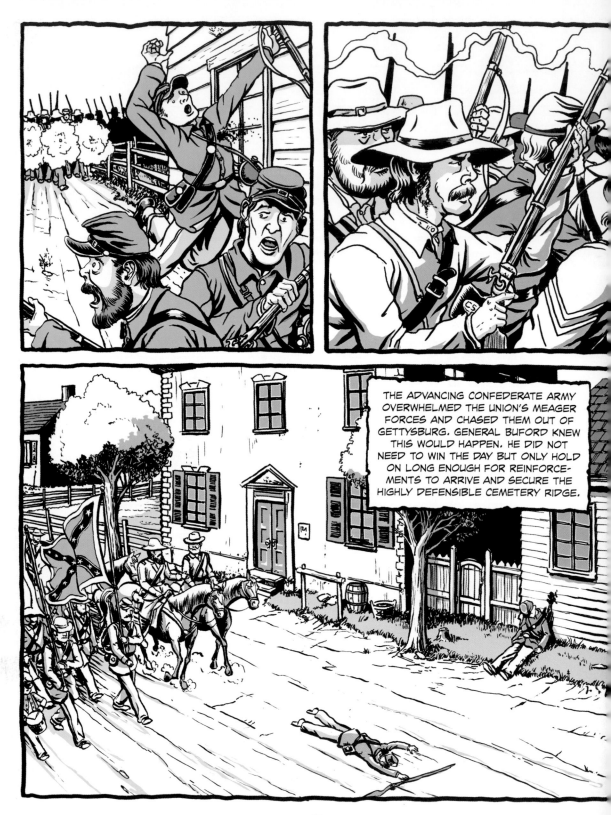

THE ADVANCING CONFEDERATE ARMY OVERWHELMED THE UNION'S MEAGER FORCES AND CHASED THEM OUT OF GETTYSBURG. GENERAL BUFORD KNEW THIS WOULD HAPPEN. HE DID NOT NEED TO WIN THE DAY BUT ONLY HOLD ON LONG ENOUGH FOR REINFORCE-MENTS TO ARRIVE AND SECURE THE HIGHLY DEFENSIBLE CEMETERY RIDGE.

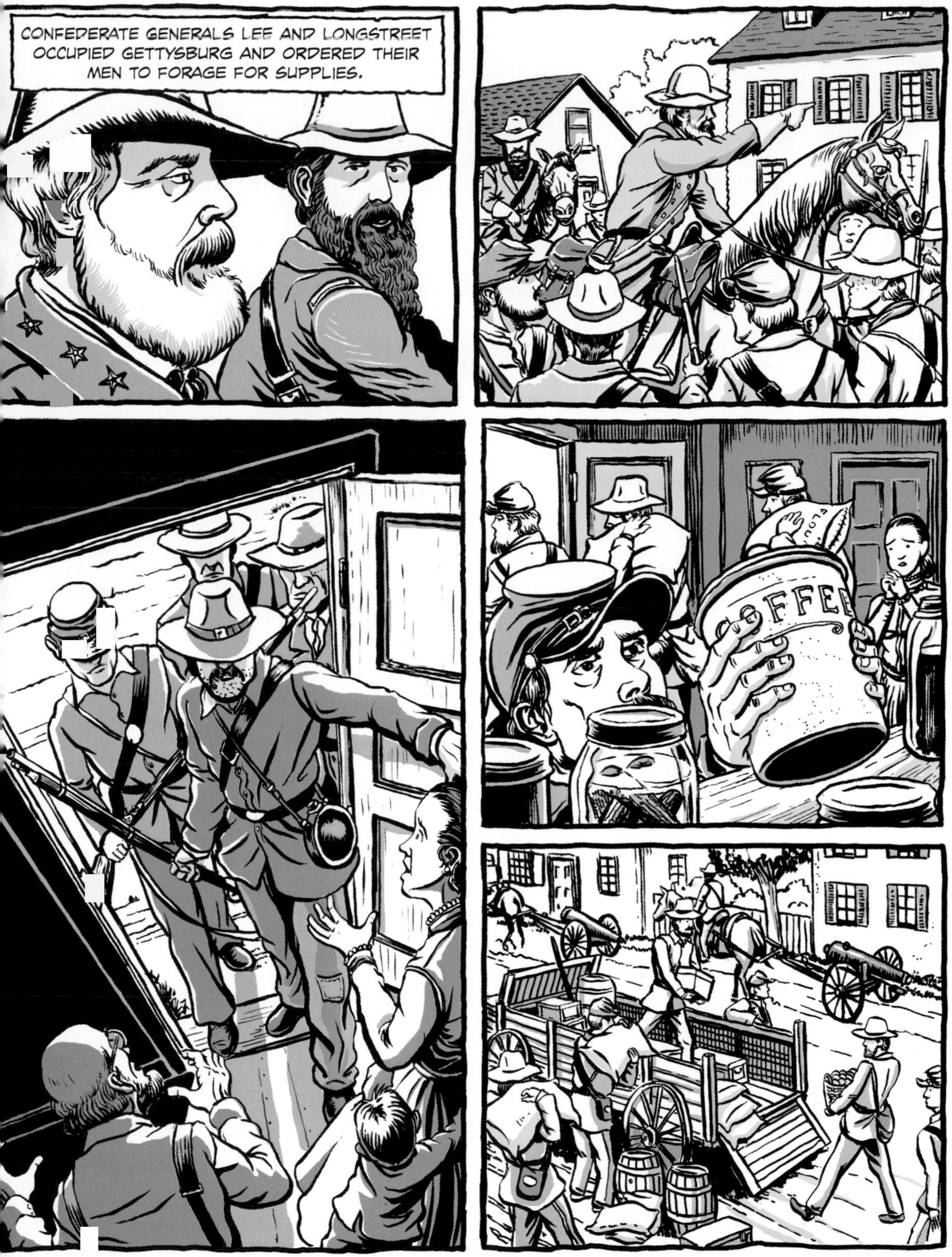
CONFEDERATE GENERALS LEE AND LONGSTREET OCCUPIED GETTYSBURG AND ORDERED THEIR MEN TO FORAGE FOR SUPPLIES.

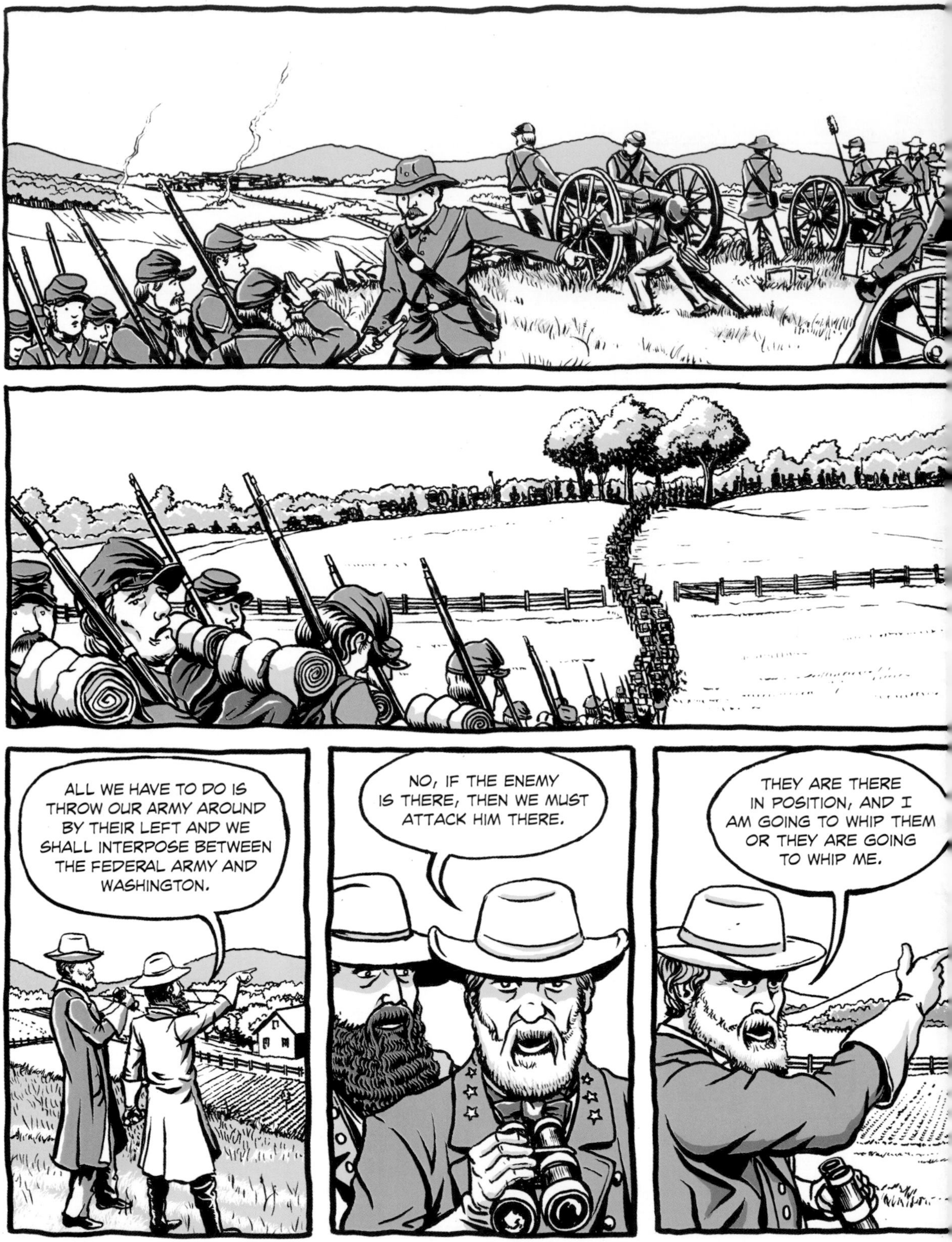
ALL WE HAVE TO DO IS THROW OUR ARMY AROUND BY THEIR LEFT AND WE SHALL INTERPOSE BETWEEN THE FEDERAL ARMY AND WASHINGTON.
NO, IF THE ENEMY IS THERE, THEN WE MUST ATTACK HIM THERE.
THEY ARE THERE IN POSITION, AND I AM GOING TO WHIP THEM OR THEY ARE GOING TO WHIP ME.

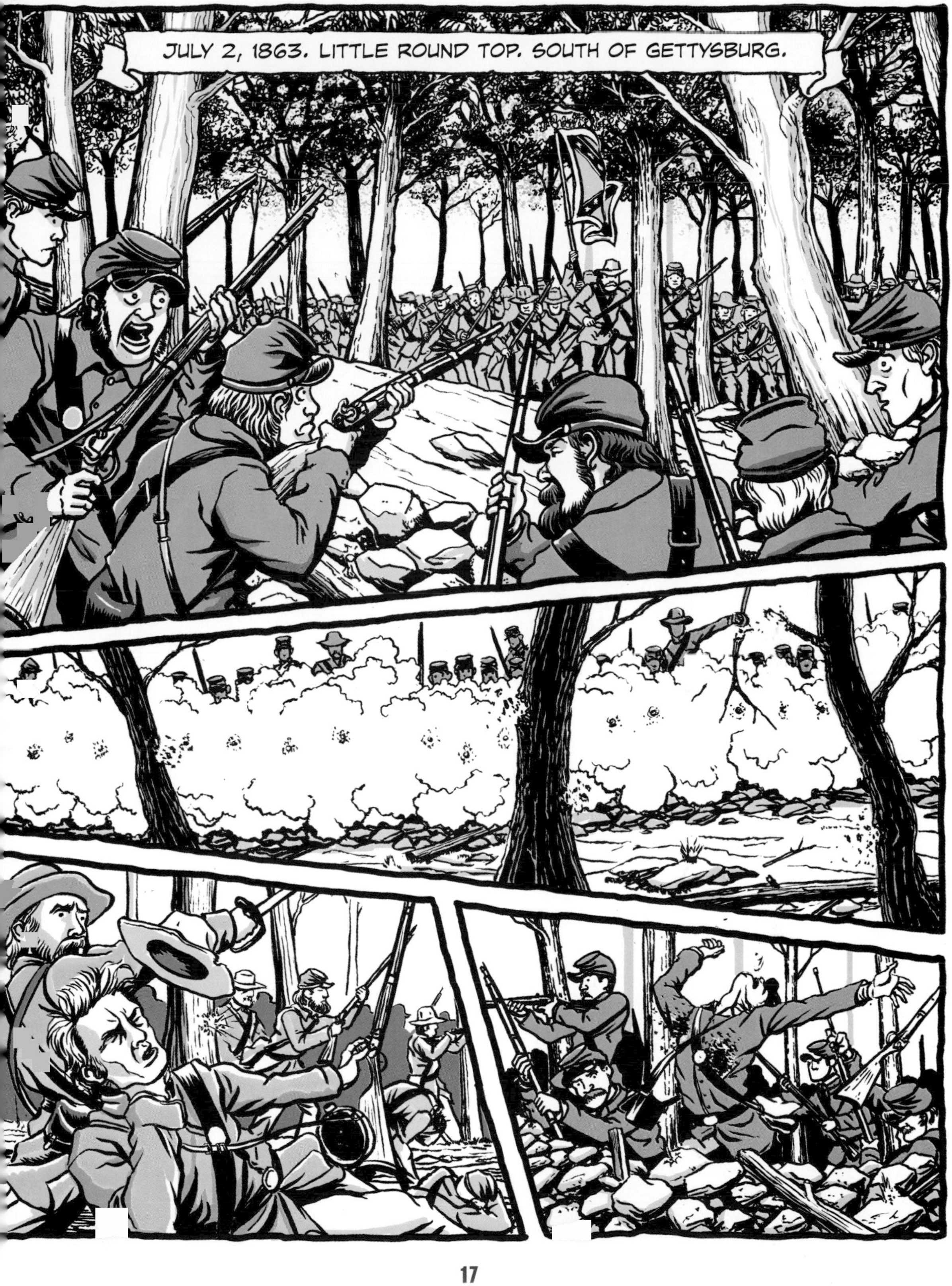
JULY 2, 1863. LITTLE ROUND TOP. SOUTH OF GETTYSBURG.

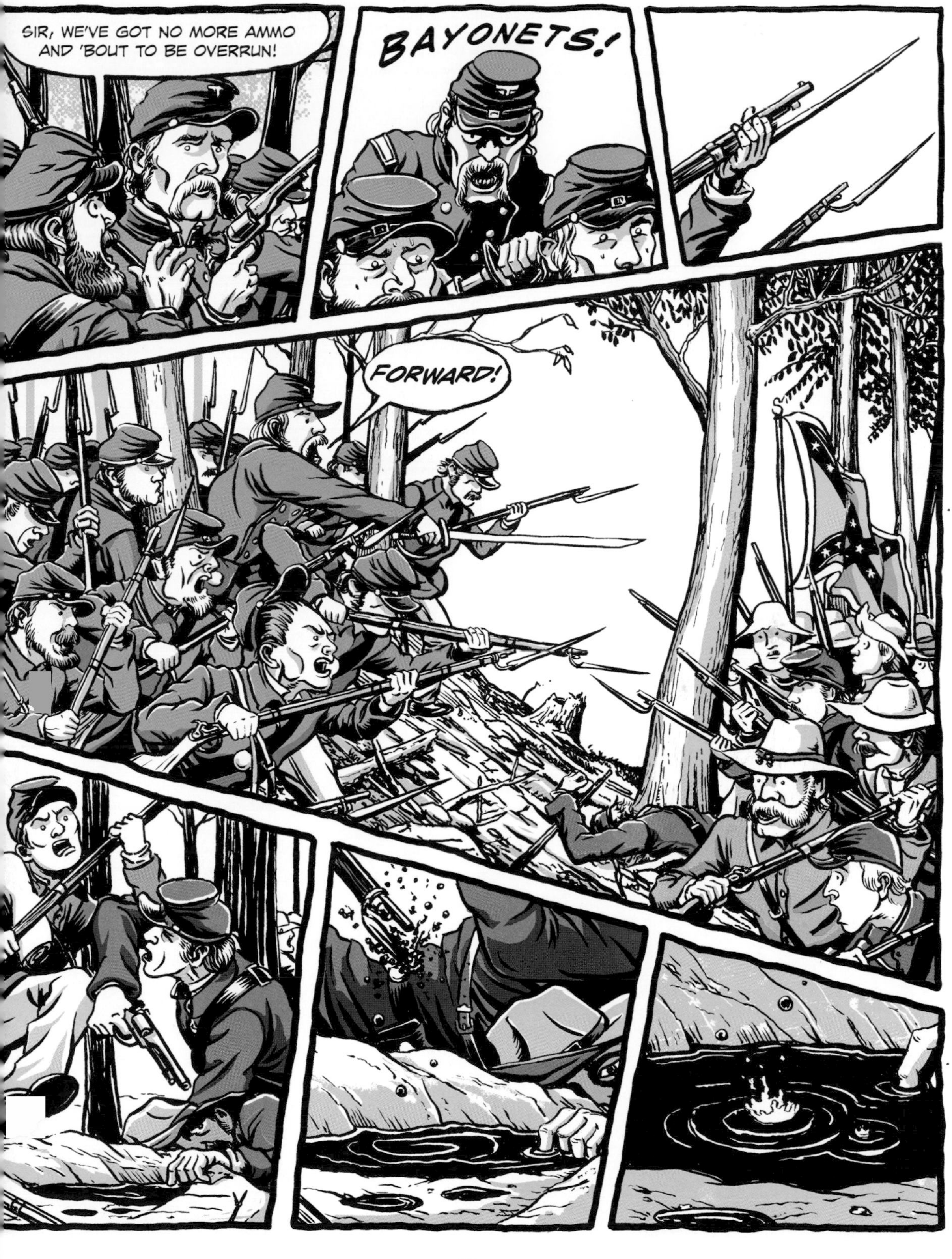
SIR, WE'VE GOT NO MORE AMMO AND 'BOUT TO BE OVERRUN!
BAYONETS!
FORWARD!

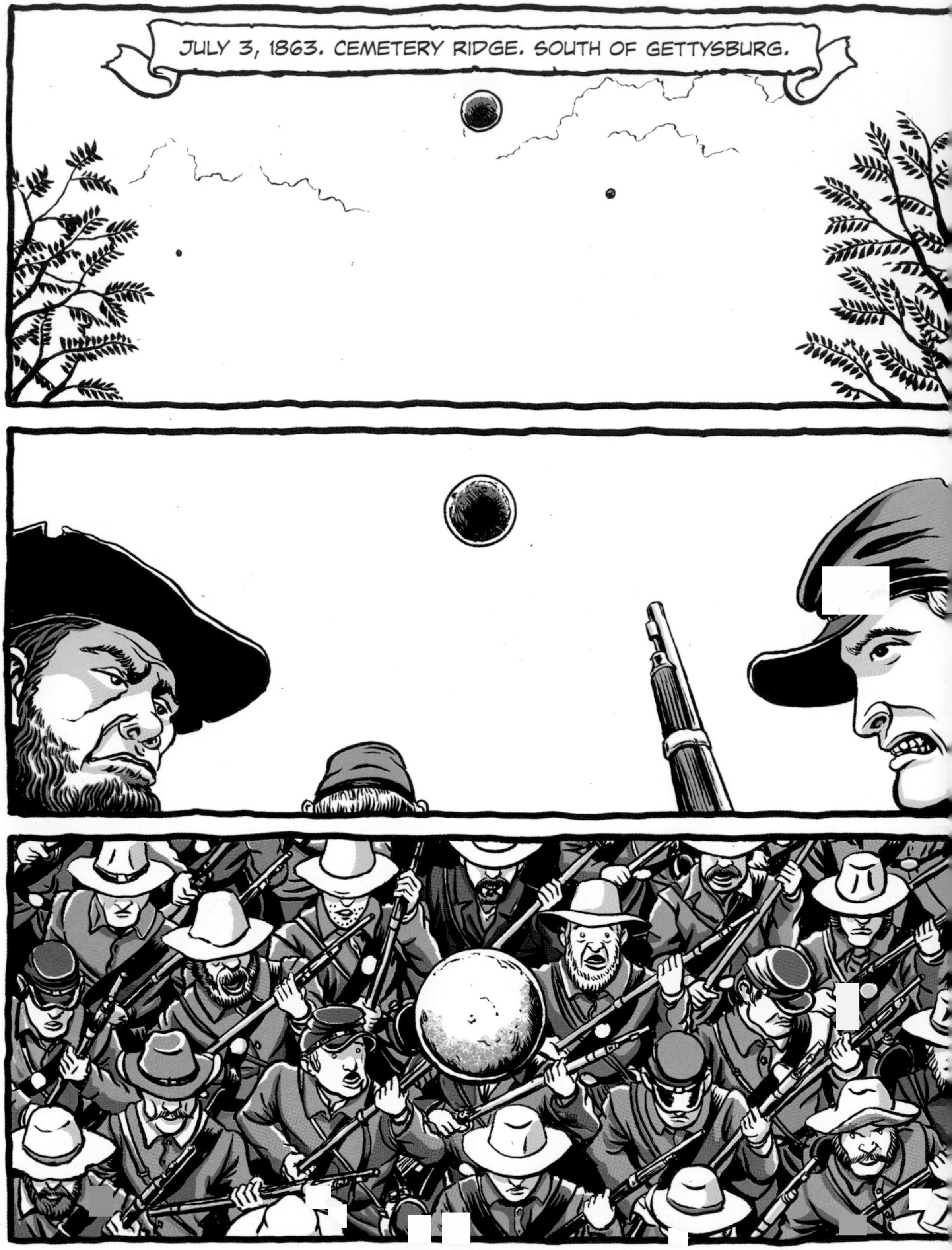
JULY 3, 1863. CEMETERY RIDGE. SOUTH OF GETTYSBURG.

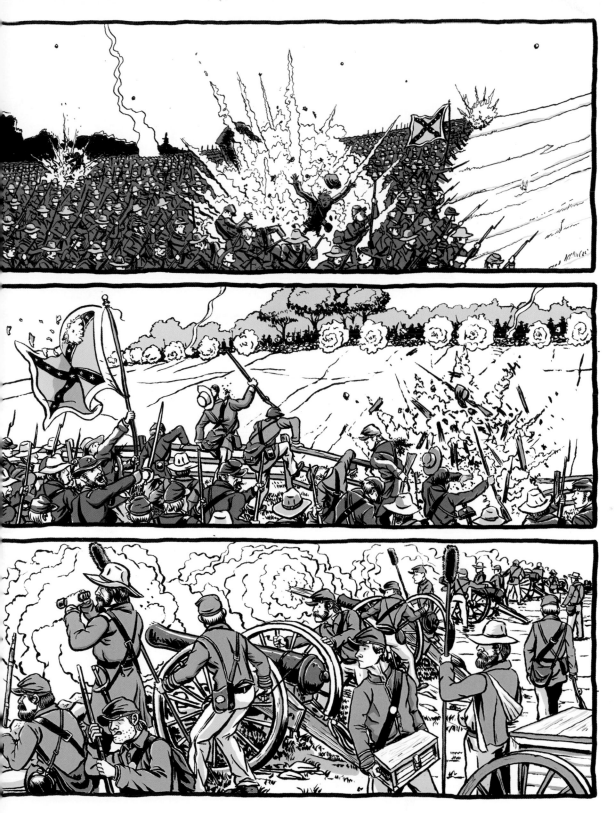

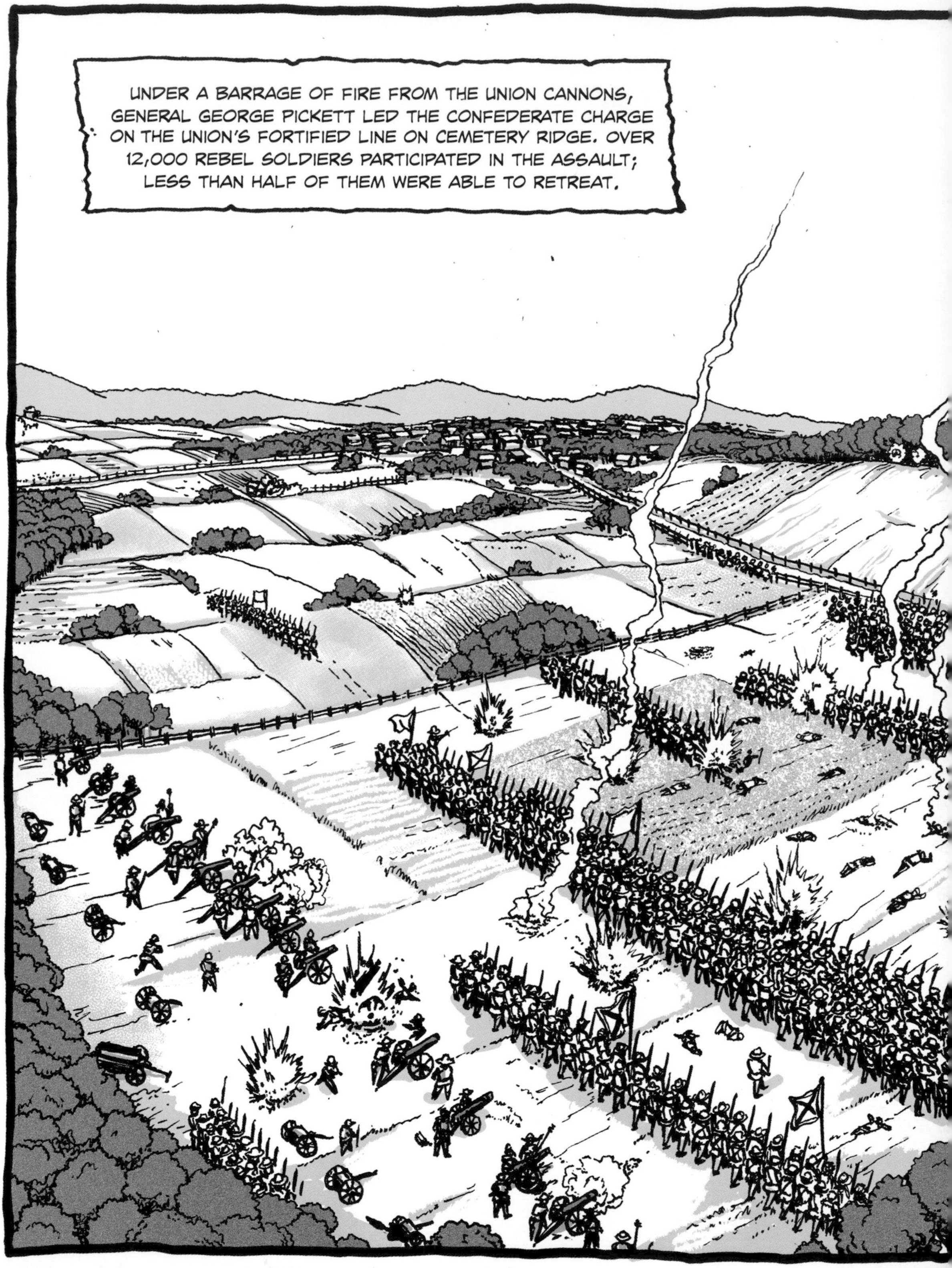
UNDER A BARRAGE OF FIRE FROM THE UNION CANNONS, GENERAL GEORGE PICKETT LED THE CONFEDERATE CHARGE ON THE UNION'S FORTIFIED LINE ON CEMETERY RIDGE. OVER 12,000 REBEL SOLDIERS PARTICIPATED IN THE ASSAULT; LESS THAN HALF OF THEM WERE ABLE TO RETREAT.

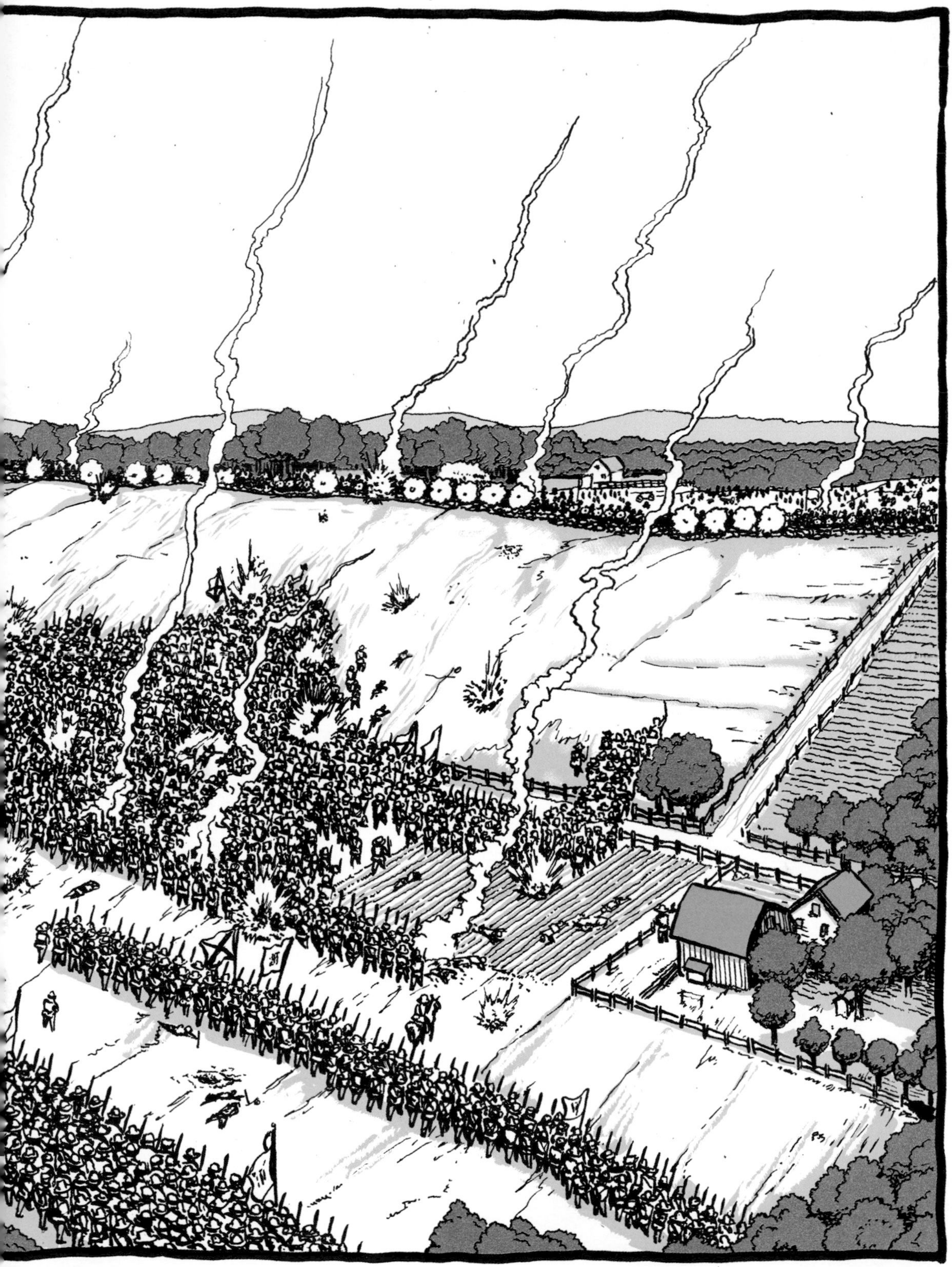

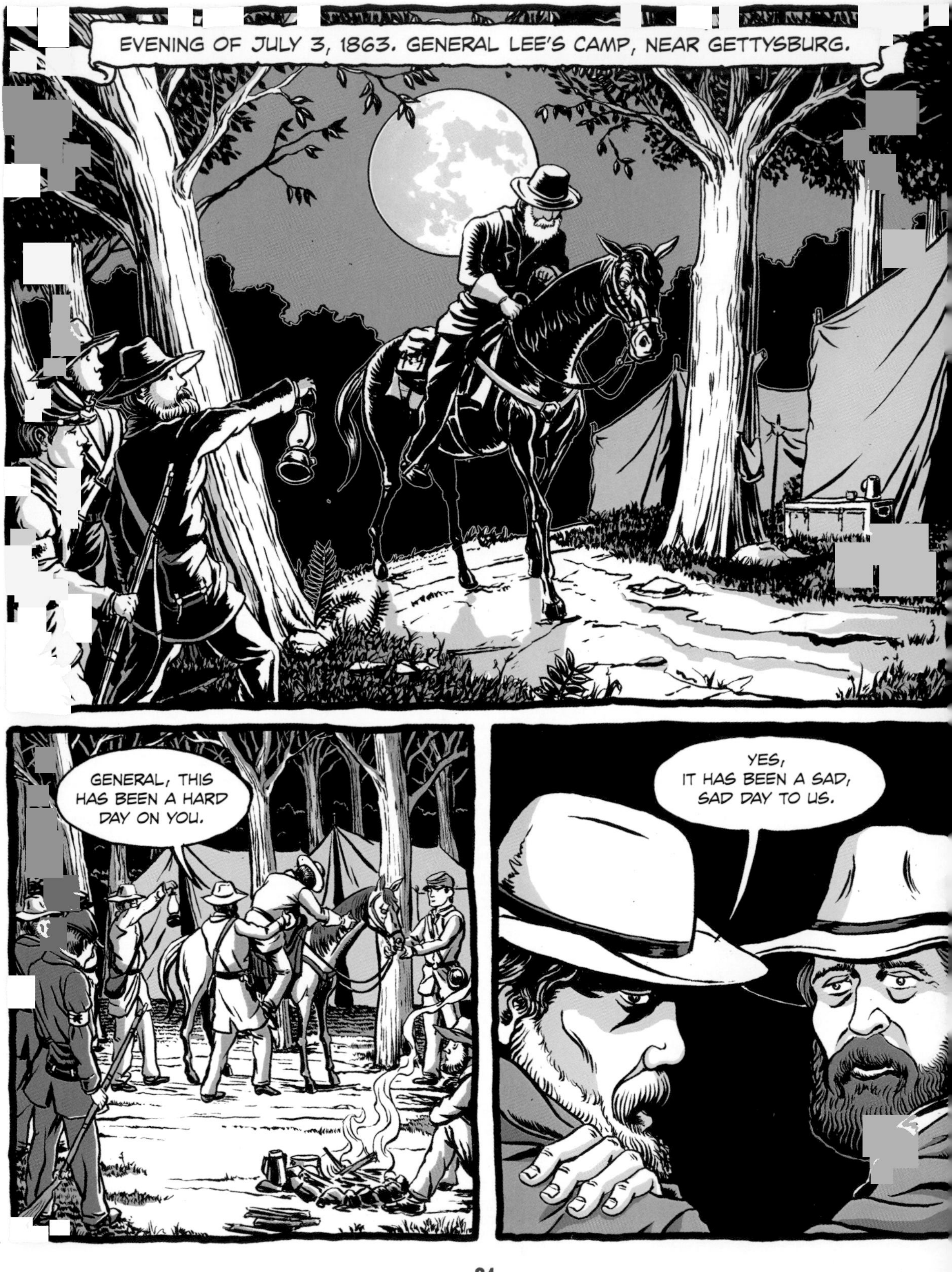
EVENING OF JULY 3, 1863. GENERAL LEE'S CAMP, NEAR GETTYSBURG.
GENERAL, THIS HAS BEEN A HARD DAY ON YOU.
YES, IT HAS BEEN A SAD, SAD DAY TO US.

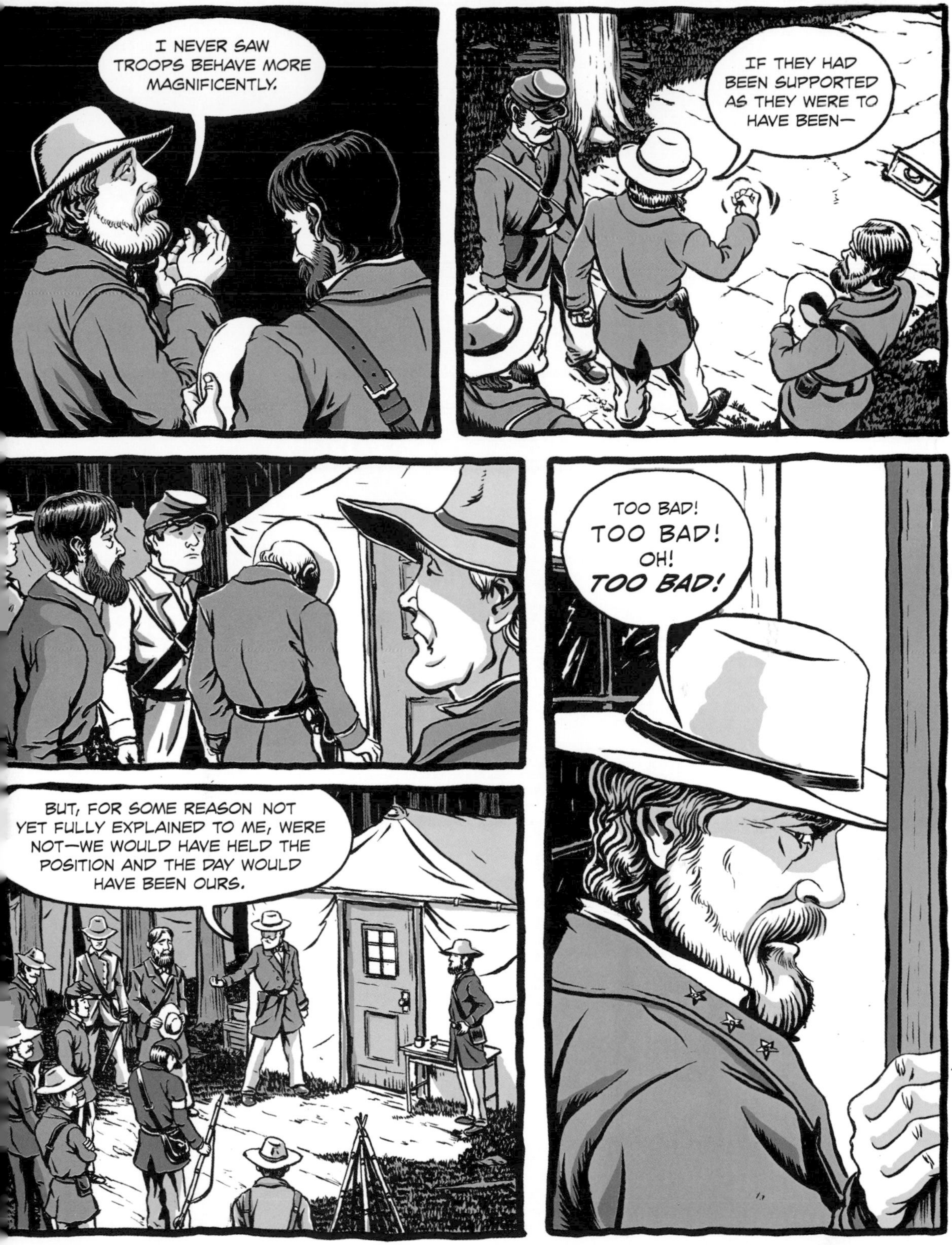
I NEVER SAW TROOPS BEHAVE MORE MAGNIFICENTLY.
IF THEY HAD BEEN SUPPORTED AS THEY WERE TO HAVE BEEN—
TOO BAD! TOO BAD! OH! TOO BAD!
BUT, FOR SOME REASON NOT YET FULLY EXPLAINED TO ME, WERE NOT—WE WOULD HAVE HELD THE POSITION AND THE DAY WOULD HAVE BEEN OURS.

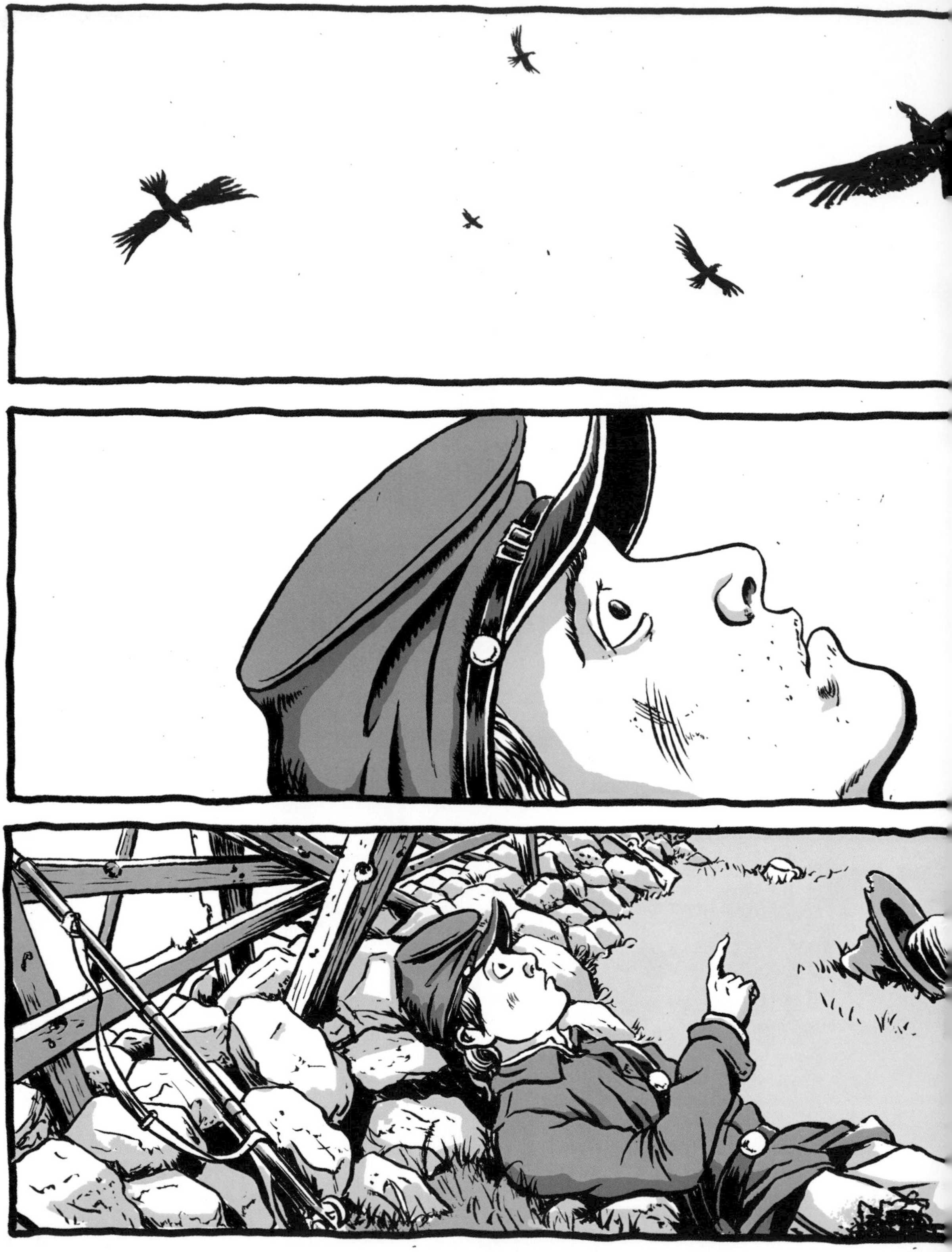

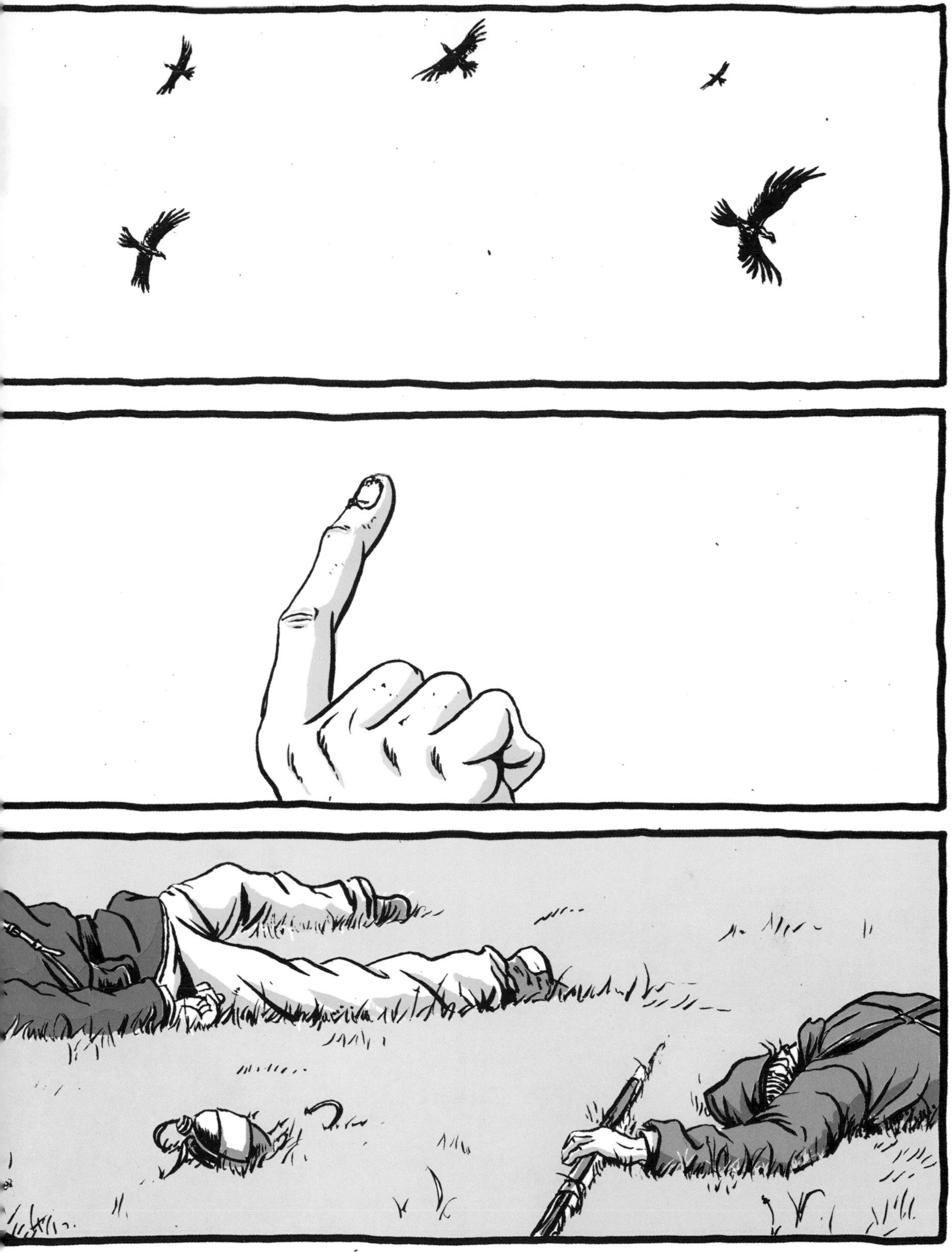

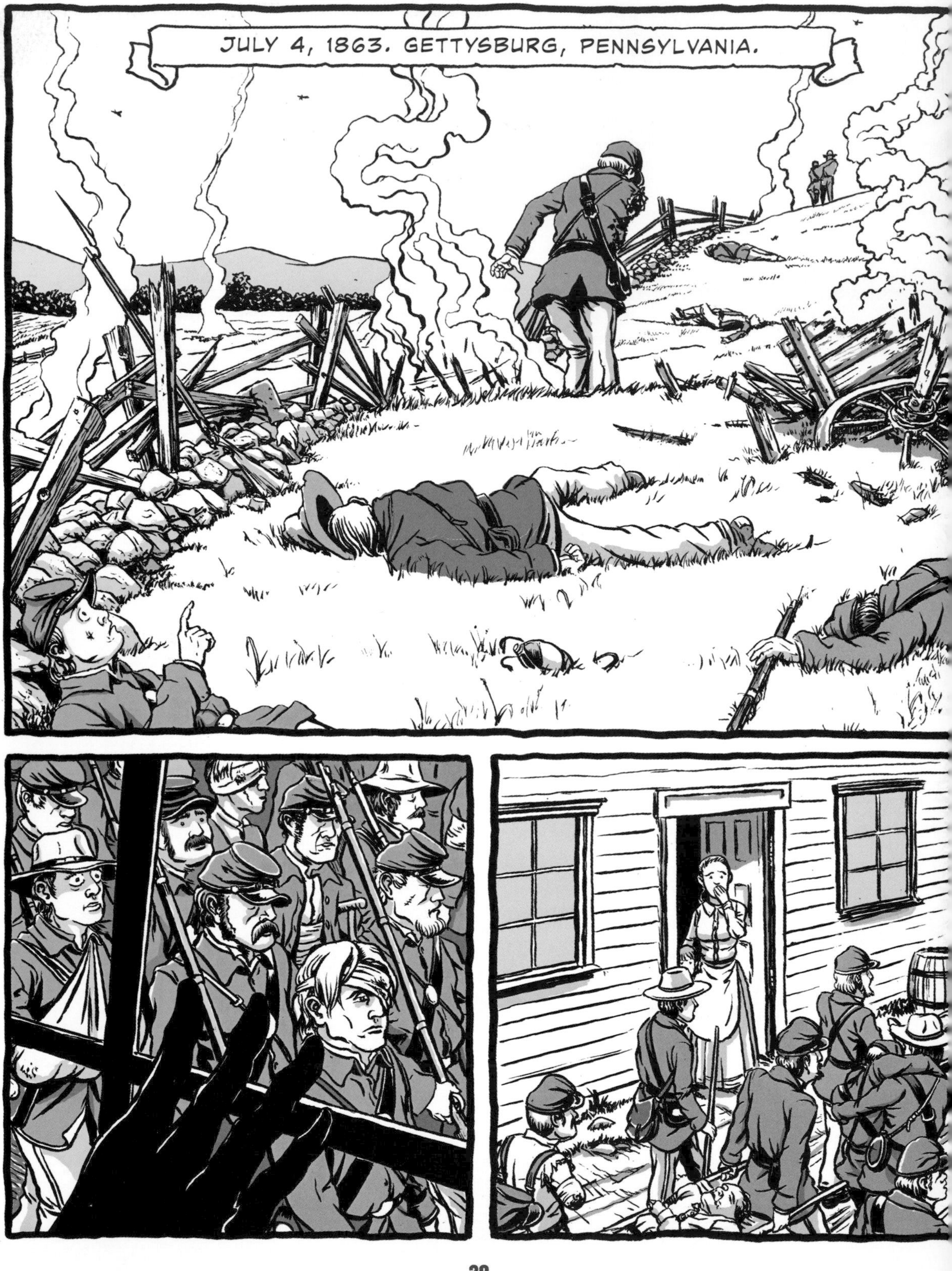
JULY 4, 1863. GETTYSBURG, PENNSYLVANIA.

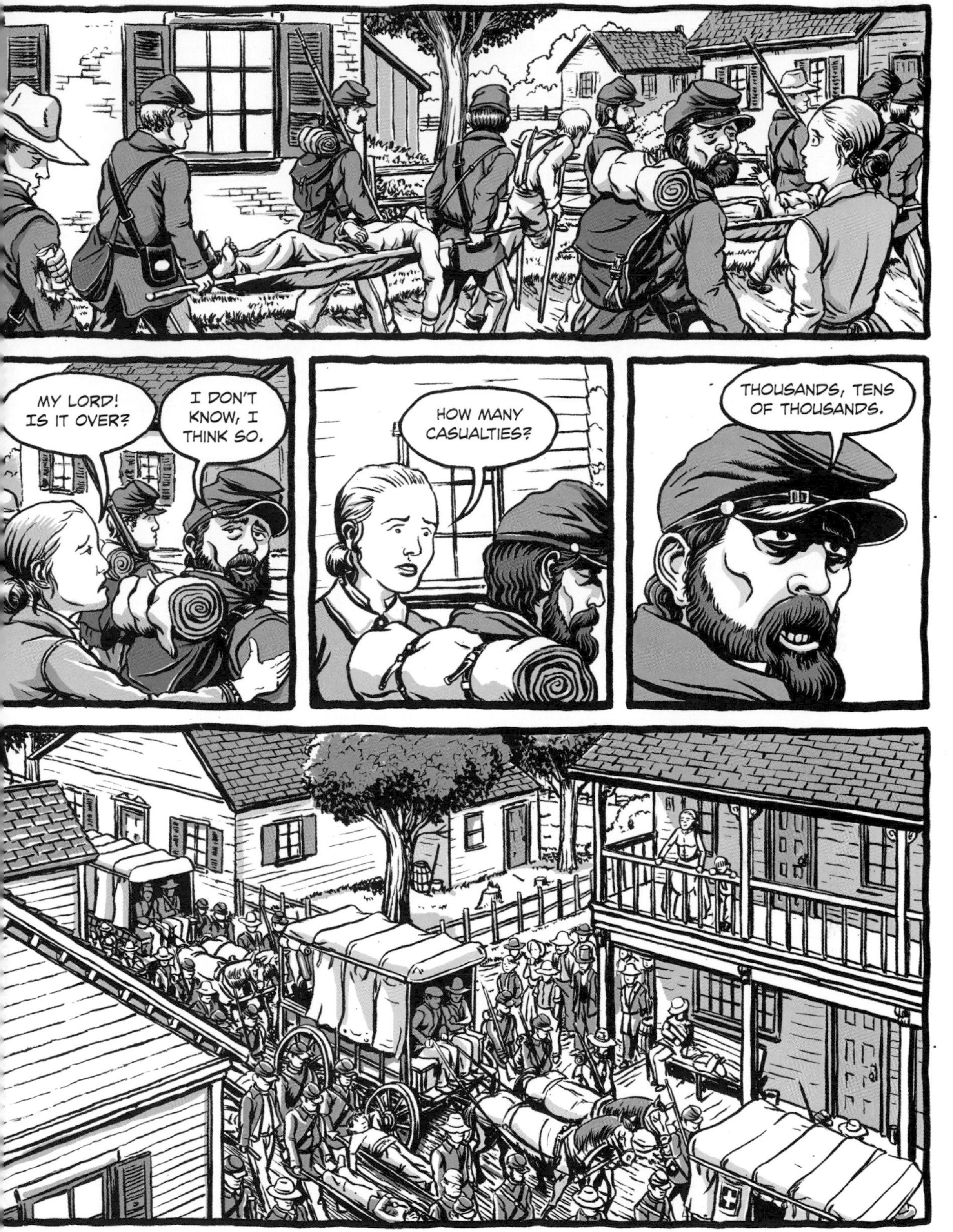
MY LORD! IS IT OVER?
I DON'T KNOW, I THINK SO.
HOW MANY CASUALTIES?
THOUSANDS, TENS OF THOUSANDS.

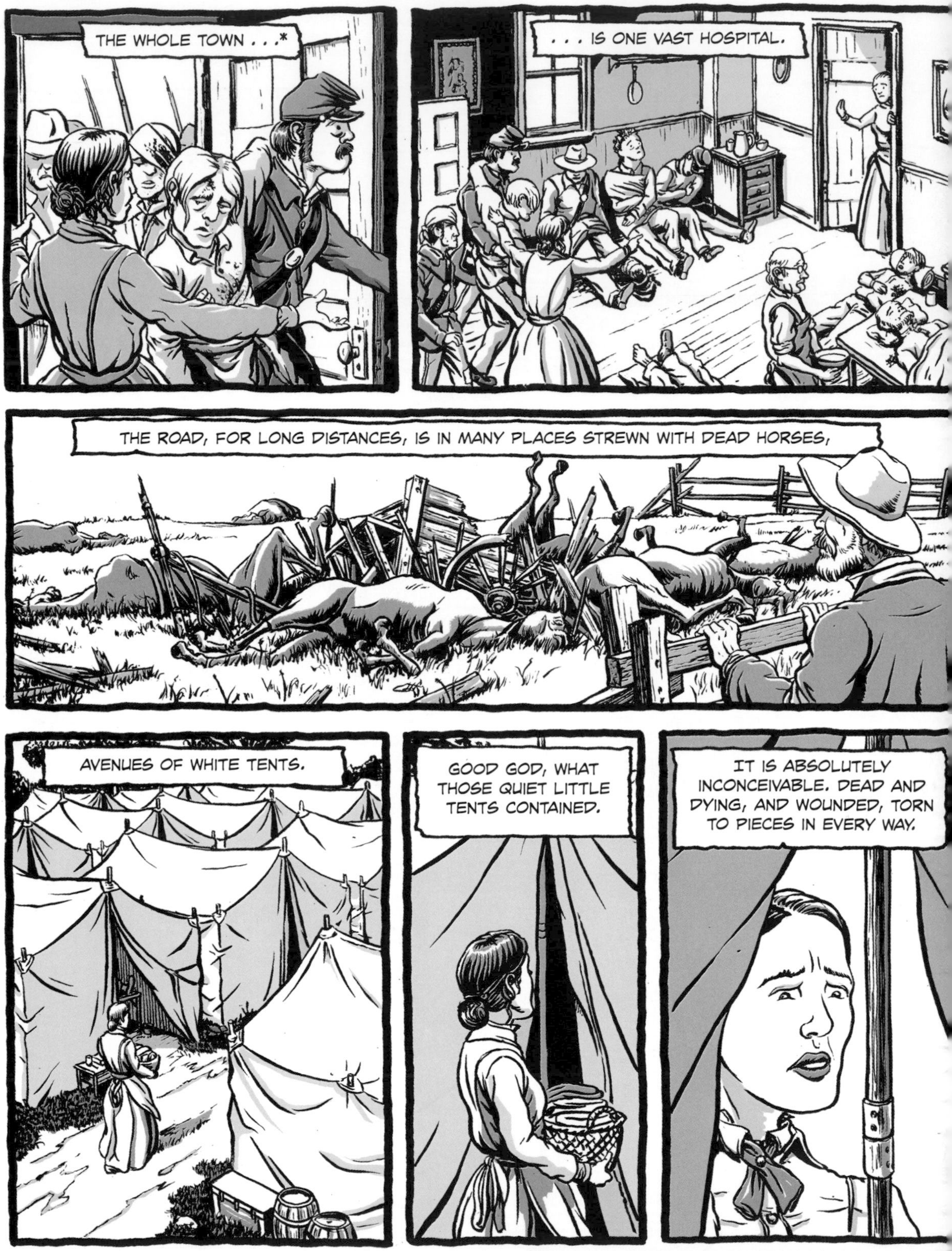
THE WHOLE TOWN . . .*
. . . IS ONE VAST HOSPITAL.
THE ROAD, FOR LONG DISTANCES, IS IN MANY PLACES STREWN WITH DEAD HORSES,
AVENUES OF WHITE TENTS.
GOOD GOD, WHAT THOSE QUIET LITTLE TENTS CONTAINED.
IT IS ABSOLUTELY INCONCEIVABLE. DEAD AND DYING, AND WOUNDED, TORN TO PIECES IN EVERY WAY.

*FROM THE LETTERS OF ELIZA FARNHAM AND EMILY SOUDE

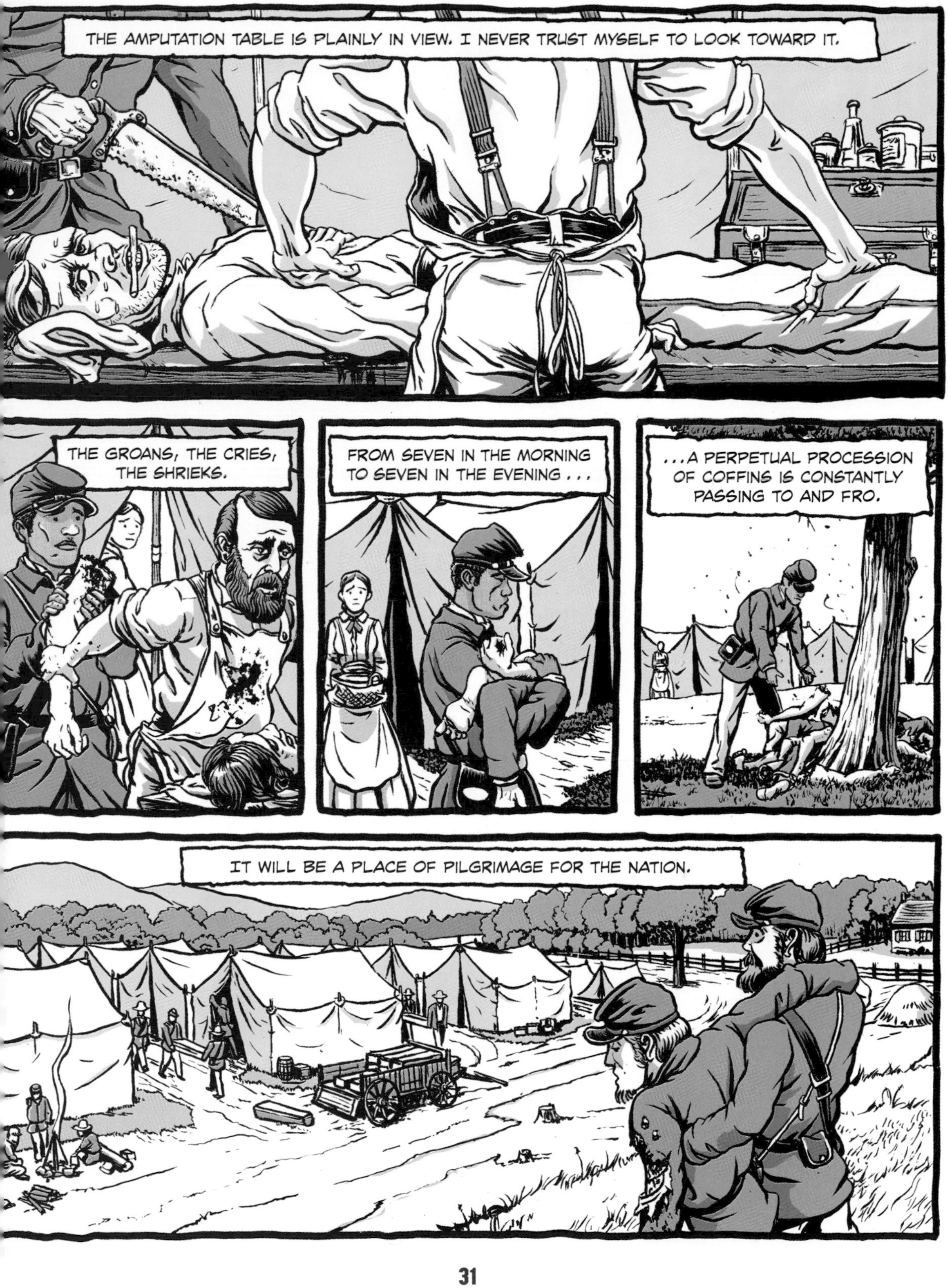
THE AMPUTATION TABLE IS PLAINLY IN VIEW. I NEVER TRUST MYSELF TO LOOK TOWARD IT.
THE GROANS, THE CRIES, THE SHRIEKS.
FROM SEVEN IN THE MORNING TO SEVEN IN THE EVENING . . .
. . . A PERPETUAL PROCESSION OF COFFINS IS CONSTANTLY PASSING TO AND FRO.
IT WILL BE A PLACE OF PILGRIMAGE FOR THE NATION.

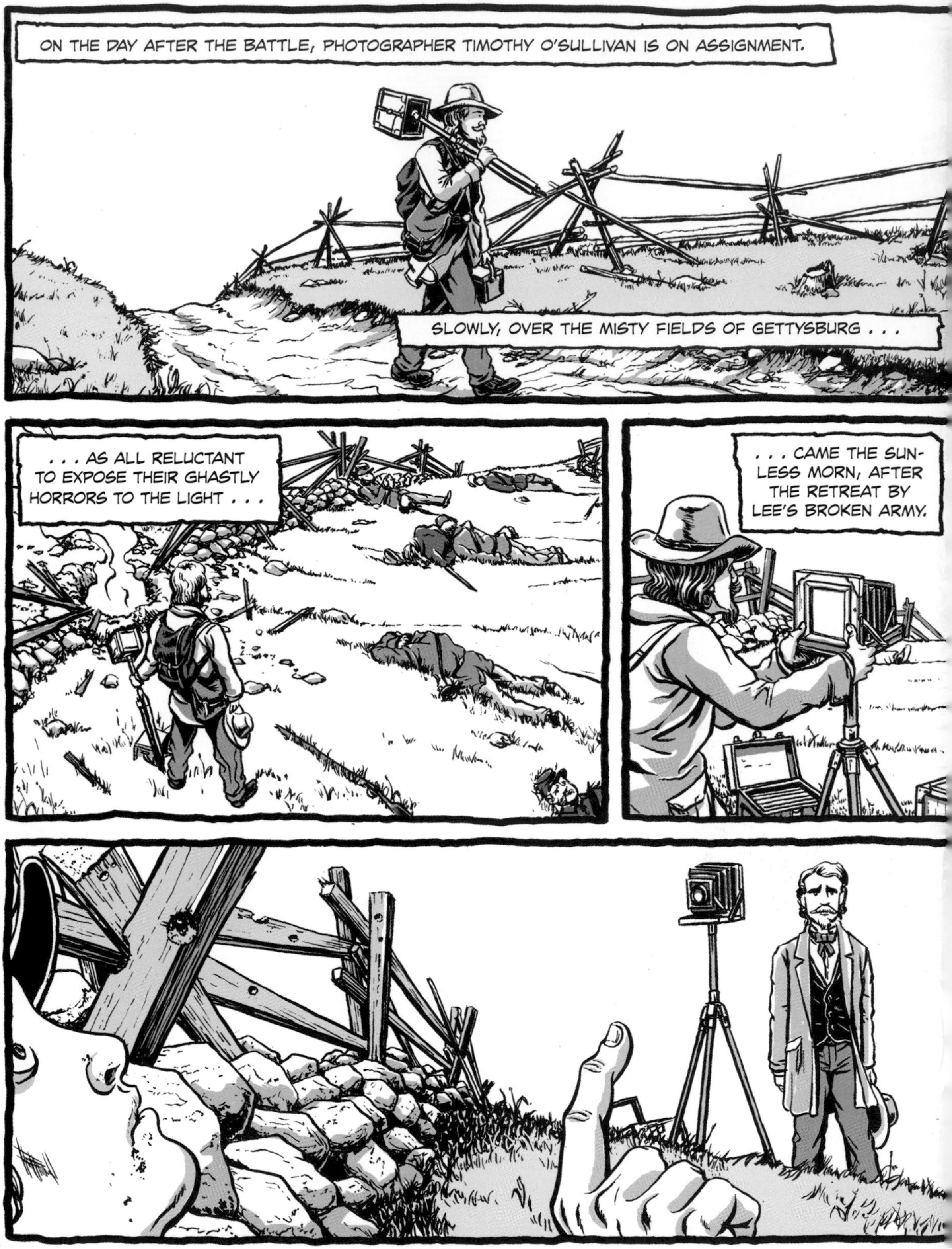
ON THE DAY AFTER THE BATTLE, PHOTOGRAPHER TIMOTHY O'SULLIVAN IS ON ASSIGNMENT.
SLOWLY, OVER THE MISTY FIELDS OF GETTYSBURG . . .
. . . AS ALL RELUCTANT TO EXPOSE THEIR GHASTLY HORRORS TO THE LIGHT . . .
. . . CAME THE SUNLESS MORN, AFTER THE RETREAT BY LEE'S BROKEN ARMY.

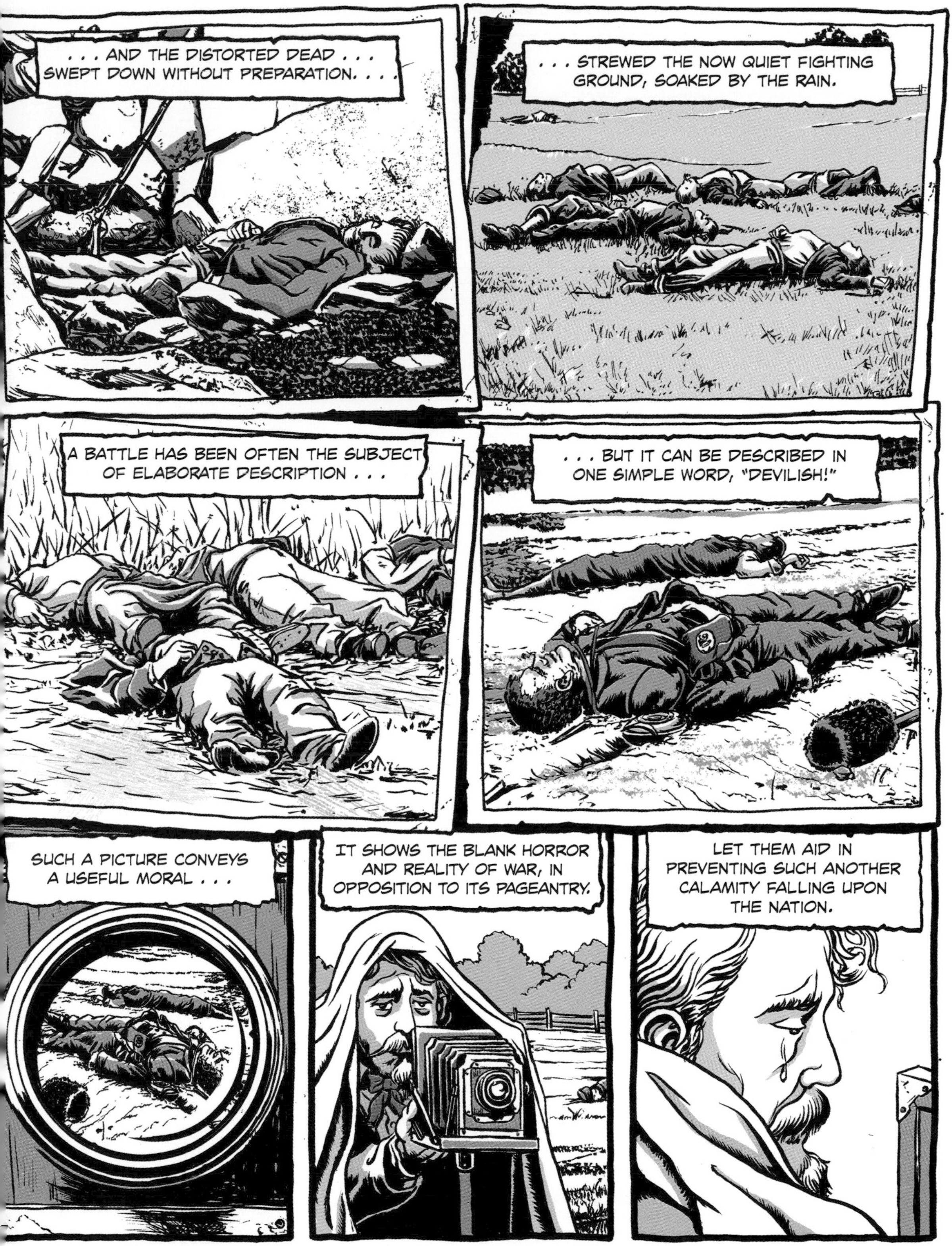
. . . AND THE DISTORTED DEAD . . . SWEPT DOWN WITHOUT PREPARATION. . . .
. . . STREWED THE NOW QUIET FIGHTING GROUND, SOAKED BY THE RAIN.
A BATTLE HAS BEEN OFTEN THE SUBJECT OF ELABORATE DESCRIPTION . . .
. . . BUT IT CAN BE DESCRIBED IN ONE SIMPLE WORD, "DEVILISH!"
SUCH A PICTURE CONVEYS A USEFUL MORAL . . .
IT SHOWS THE BLANK HORROR AND REALITY OF WAR, IN OPPOSITION TO ITS PAGEANTRY.
LET THEM AID IN PREVENTING SUCH ANOTHER CALAMITY FALLING UPON THE NATION.

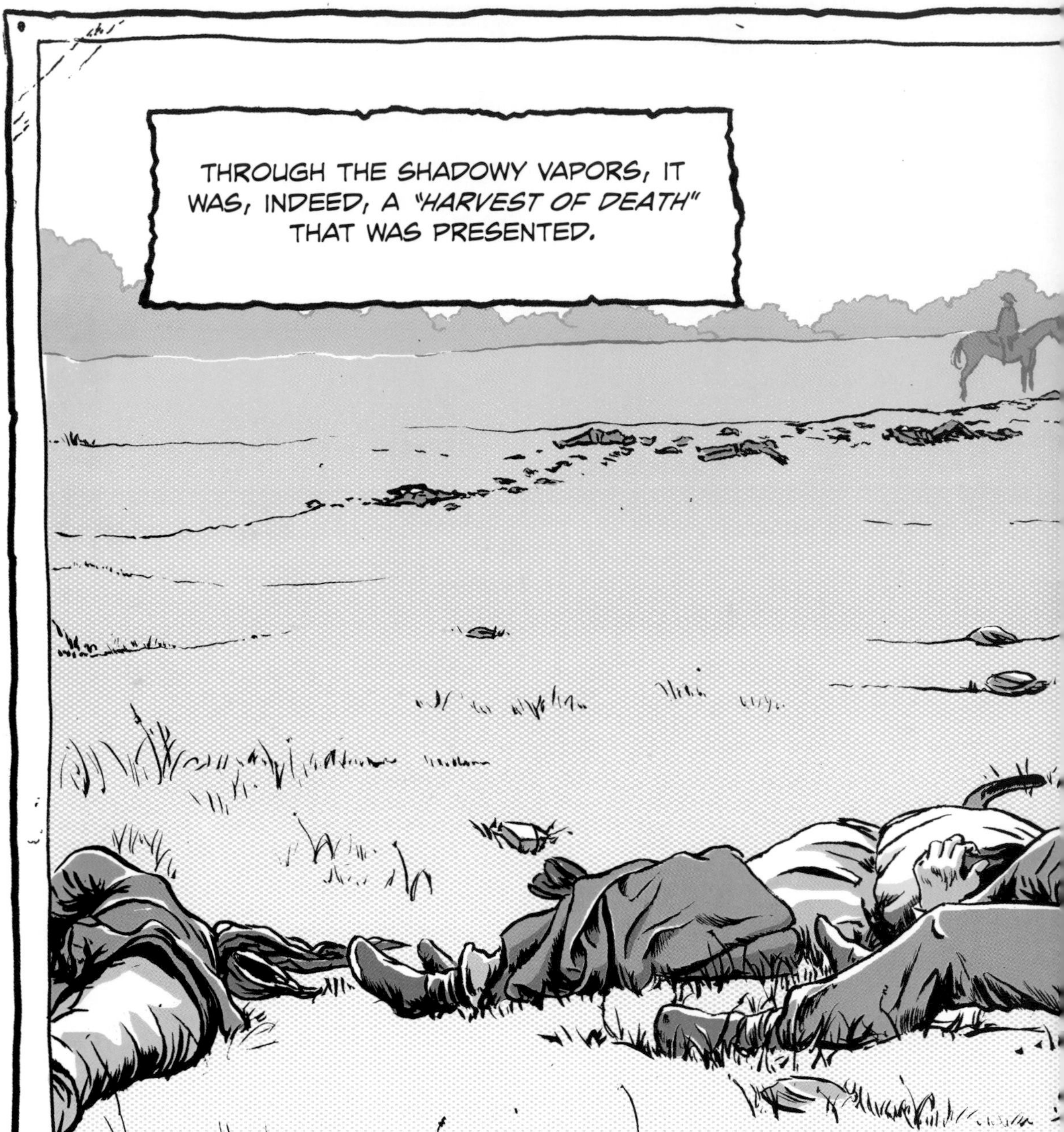
THROUGH THE SHADOWY VAPORS, IT WAS, INDEED, A "HARVEST OF DEATH" THAT WAS PRESENTED.

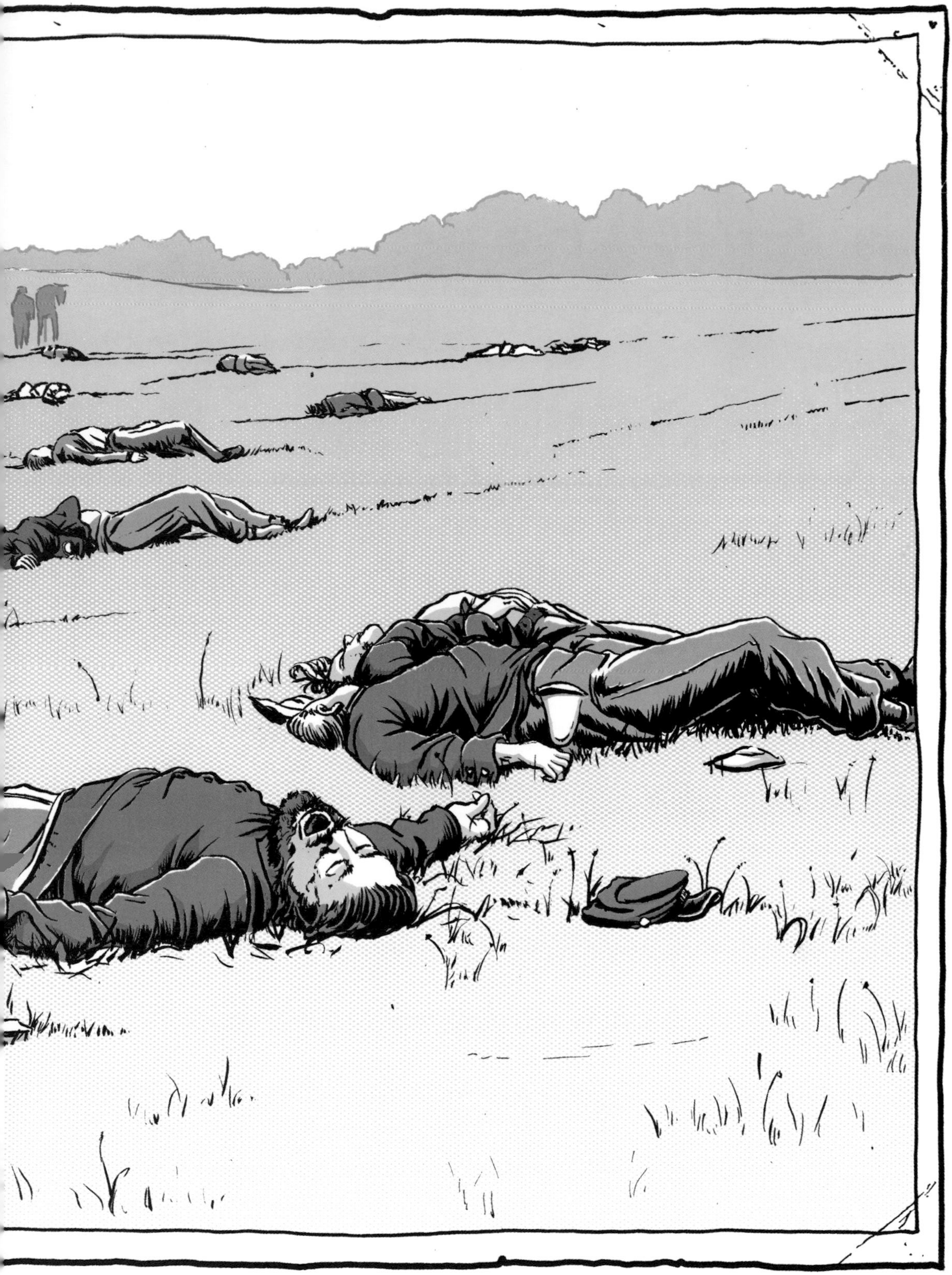

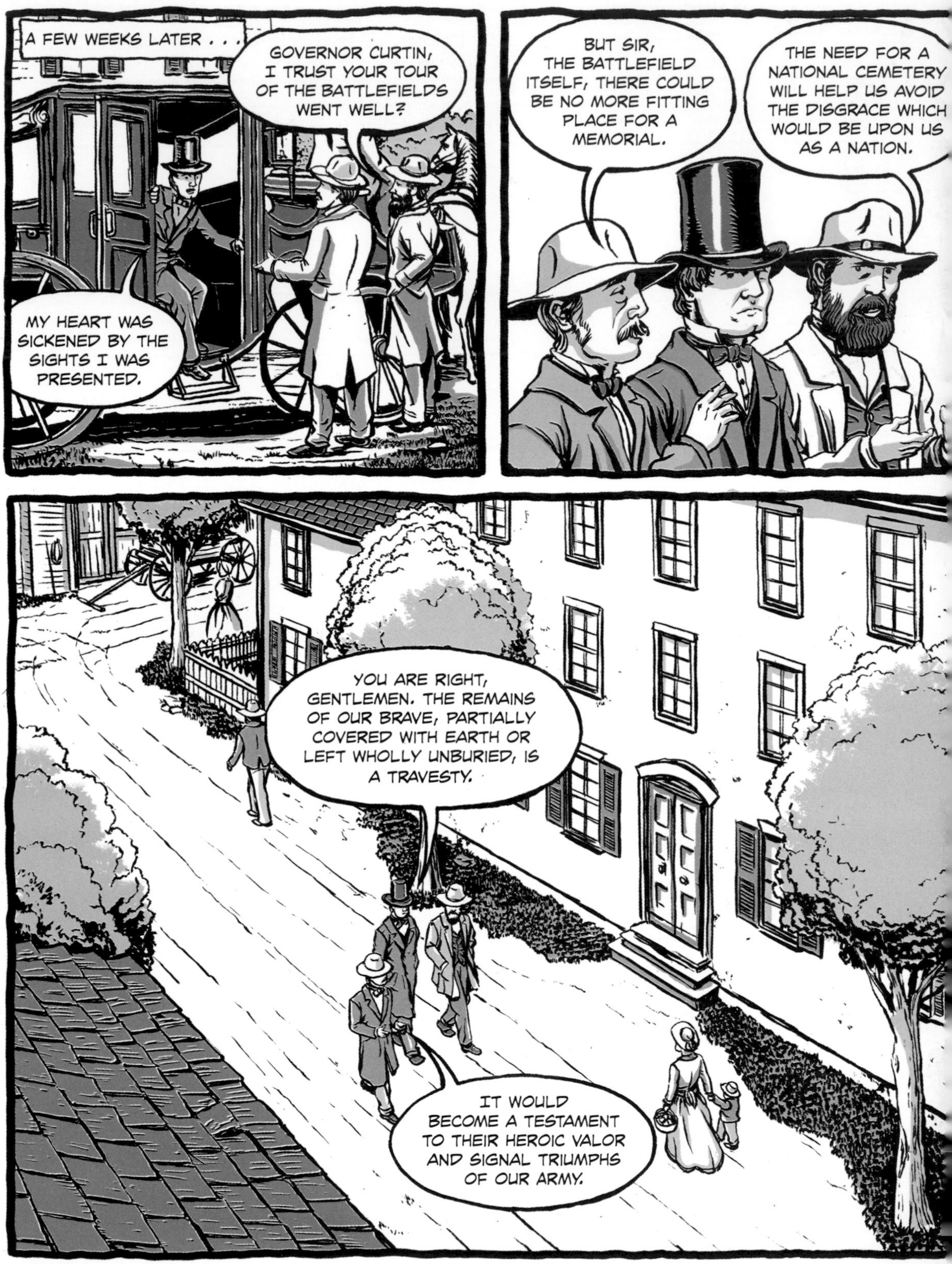
A FEW WEEKS LATER . . .
GOVERNOR CURTIN, I TRUST YOUR TOUR OF THE BATTLEFIELDS WENT WELL?
MY HEART WAS SICKENED BY THE SIGHTS I WAS PRESENTED.
BUT SIR, THE BATTLEFIELD ITSELF, THERE COULD BE NO MORE FITTING PLACE FOR A MEMORIAL.
THE NEED FOR A NATIONAL CEMETERY WILL HELP US AVOID THE DISGRACE WHICH WOULD BE UPON US AS A NATION.
YOU ARE RIGHT, GENTLEMEN. THE REMAINS OF OUR BRAVE, PARTIALLY COVERED WITH EARTH OR LEFT WHOLLY UNBURIED, IS A TRAVESTY.
IT WOULD BECOME A TESTAMENT TO THEIR HEROIC VALOR AND SIGNAL TRIUMPHS OF OUR ARMY.

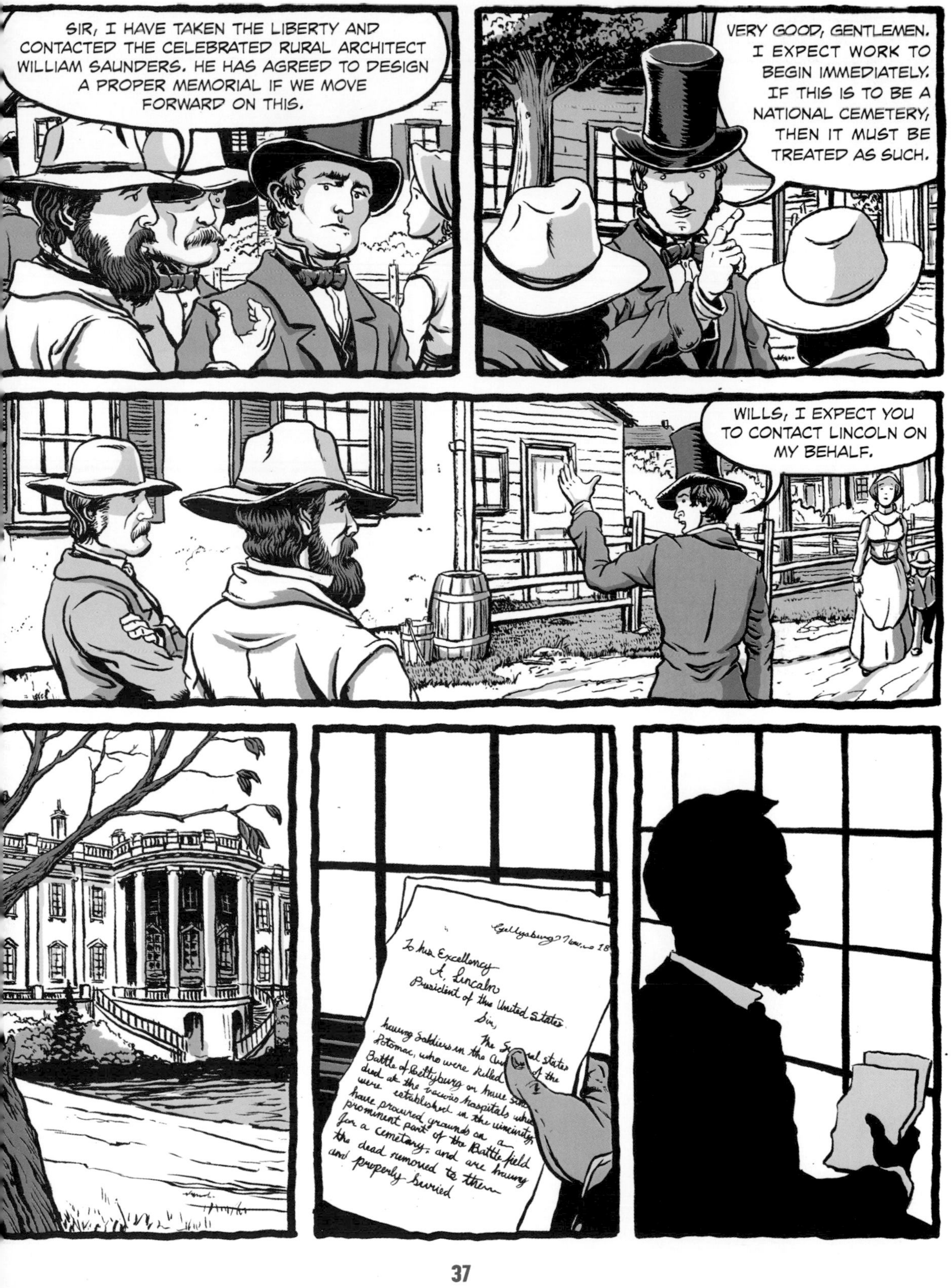
SIR, I HAVE TAKEN THE LIBERTY AND CONTACTED THE CELEBRATED RURAL ARCHITECT WILLIAM SAUNDERS. HE HAS AGREED TO DESIGN A PROPER MEMORIAL IF WE MOVE FORWARD ON THIS.
VERY GOOD, GENTLEMEN. I EXPECT WORK TO BEGIN IMMEDIATELY. IF THIS IS TO BE A NATIONAL CEMETERY, THEN IT MUST BE TREATED AS SUCH.
WILLS, I EXPECT YOU TO CONTACT LINCOLN ON MY BEHALF.
To his Excellency
A. Lincoln
President of the United States
Sir,
the dead removed to them
and properly buried

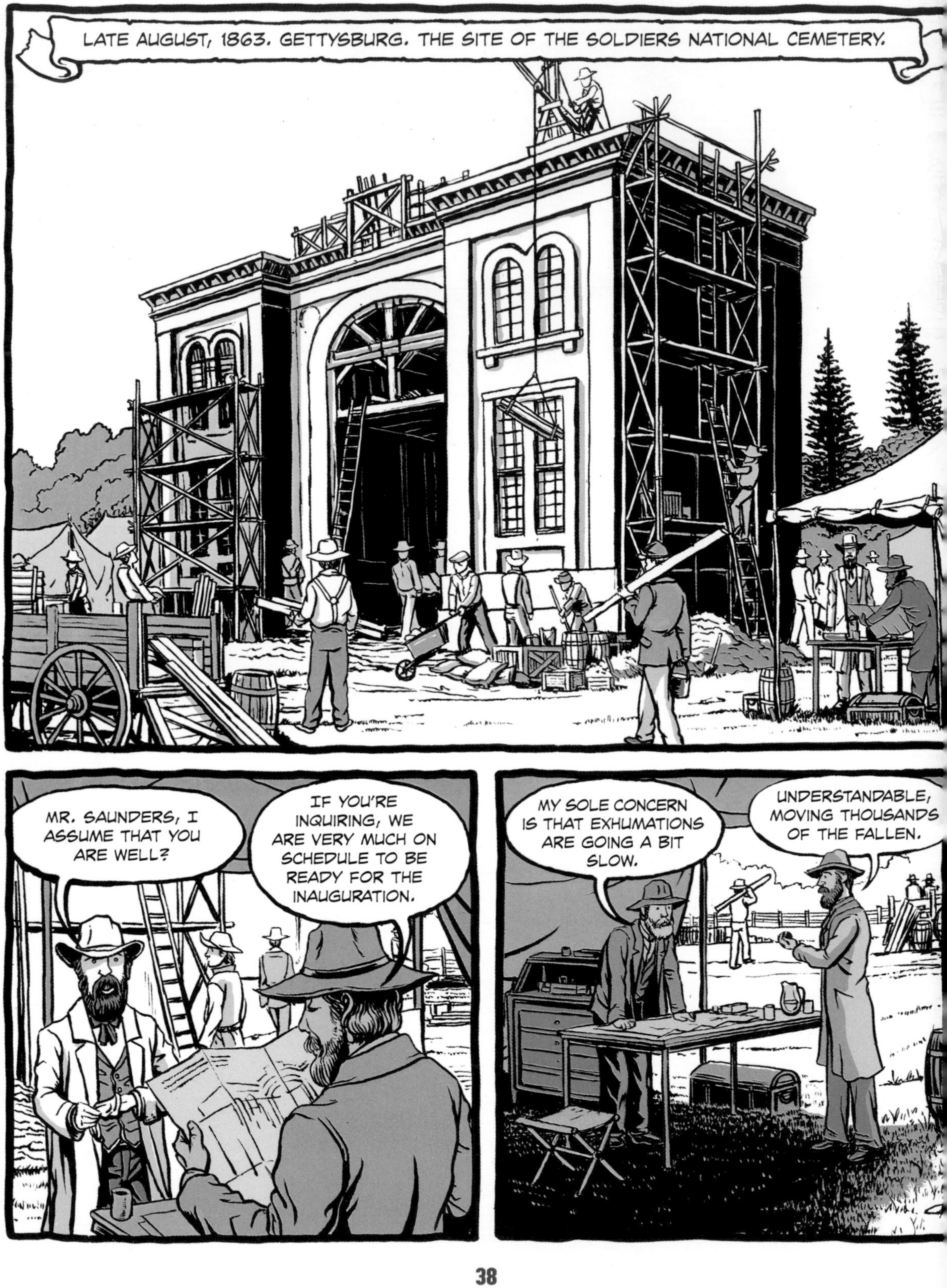

LATE AUGUST, 1863. GETTYSBURG. THE SITE OF THE SOLDIERS NATIONAL CEMETERY.
MR. SAUNDERS, I ASSUME THAT YOU ARE WELL?
IF YOU'RE INQUIRING, WE ARE VERY MUCH ON SCHEDULE TO BE READY FOR THE INAUGURATION.
MY SOLE CONCERN IS THAT EXHUMATIONS ARE GOING A BIT SLOW.
UNDERSTANDABLE, MOVING THOUSANDS OF THE FALLEN.

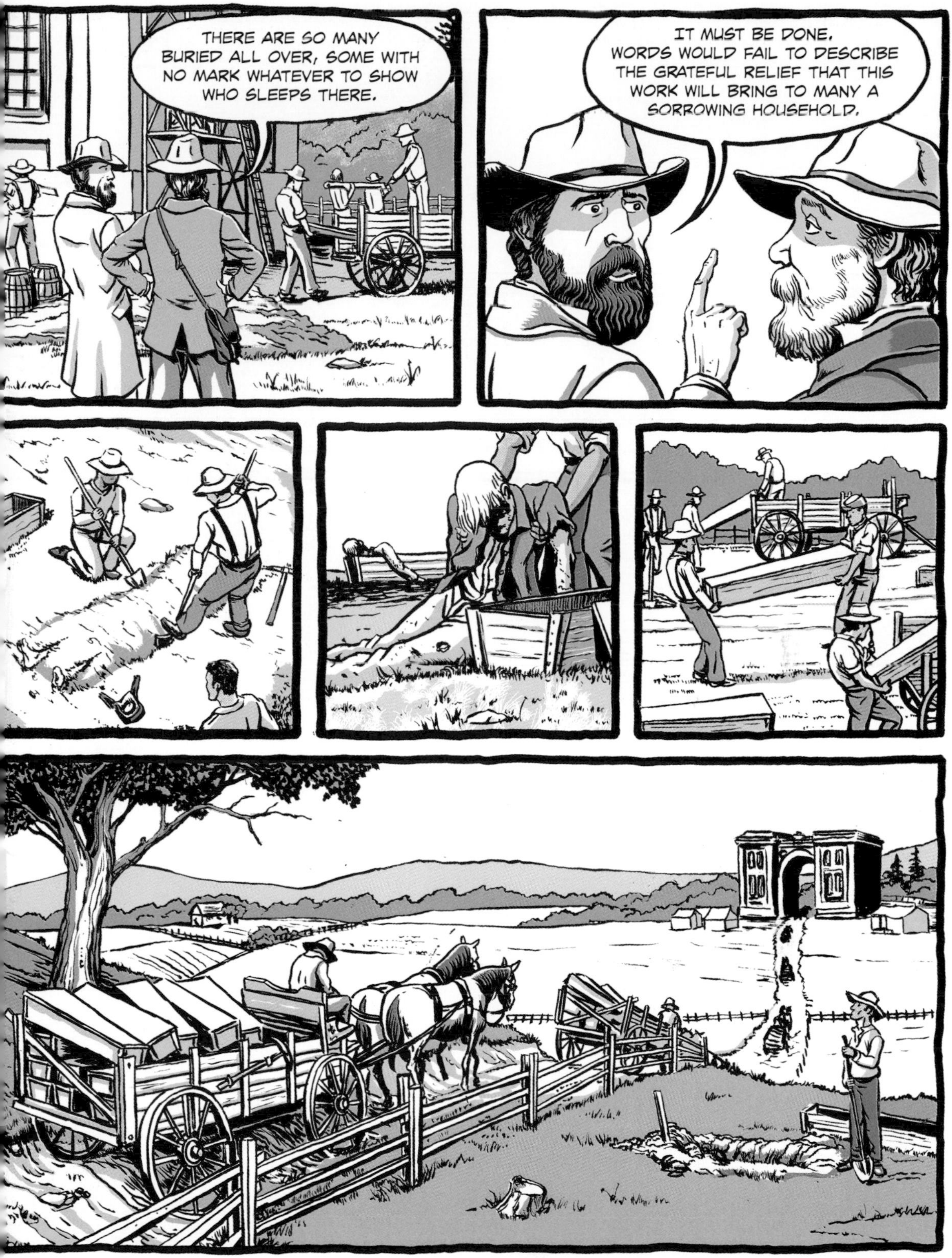
THERE ARE SO MANY BURIED ALL OVER, SOME WITH NO MARK WHATEVER TO SHOW WHO SLEEPS THERE.
IT MUST BE DONE. WORDS WOULD FAIL TO DESCRIBE THE GRATEFUL RELIEF THAT THIS WORK WILL BRING TO MANY A SORROWING HOUSEHOLD.

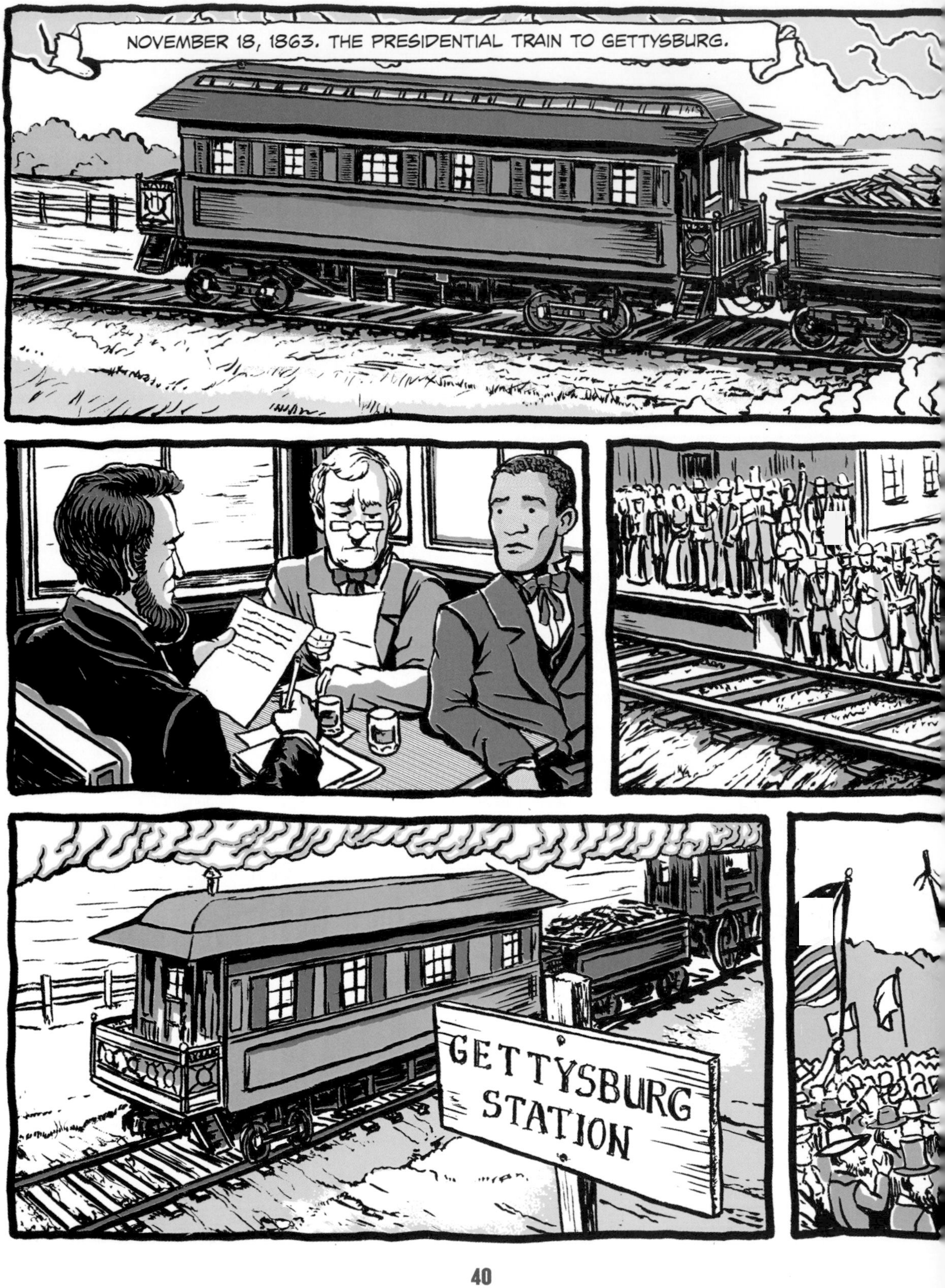
NOVEMBER 18, 1863. THE PRESIDENTIAL TRAIN TO GETTYSBURG.
GETTYSBURG STATION

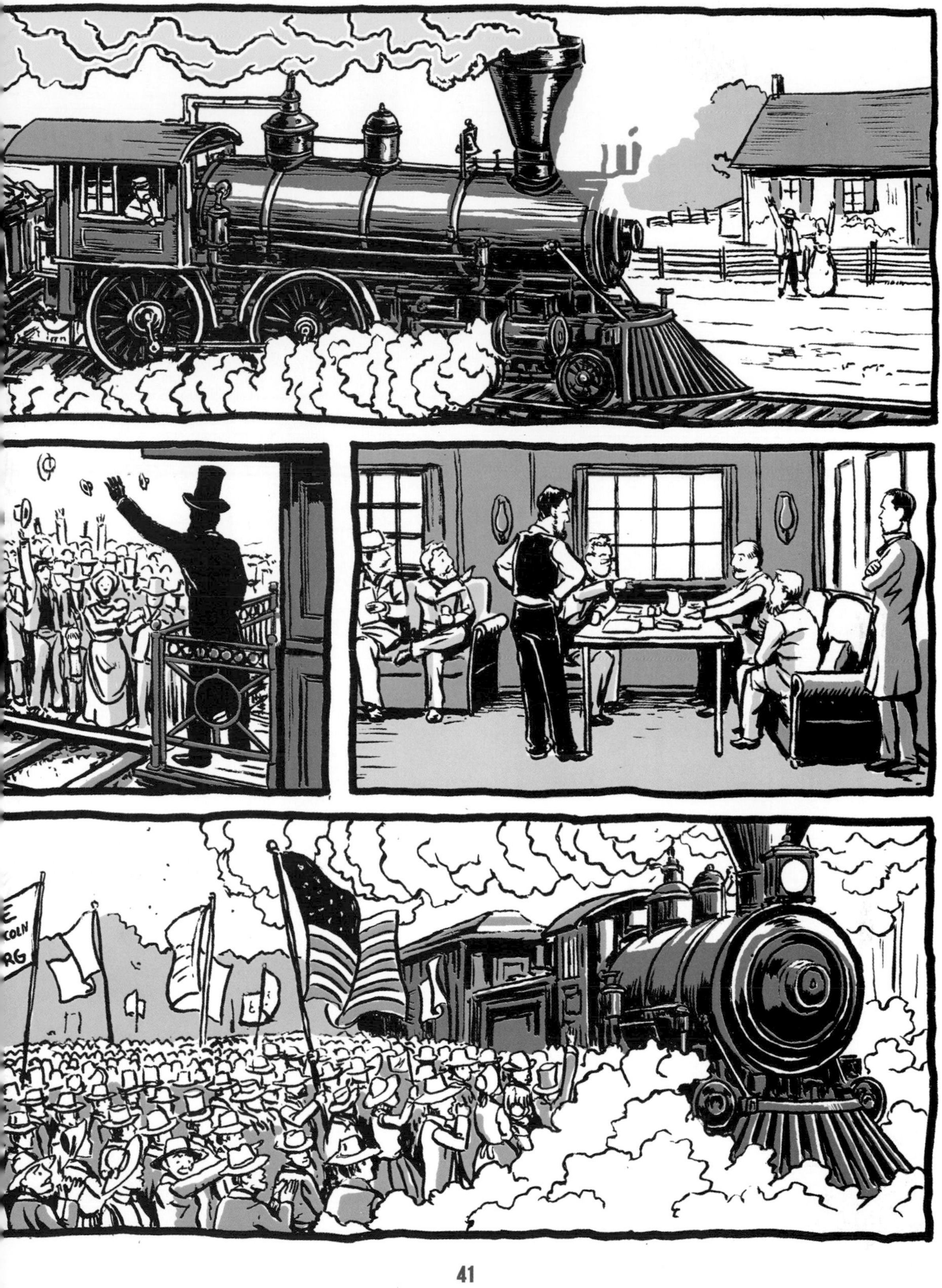

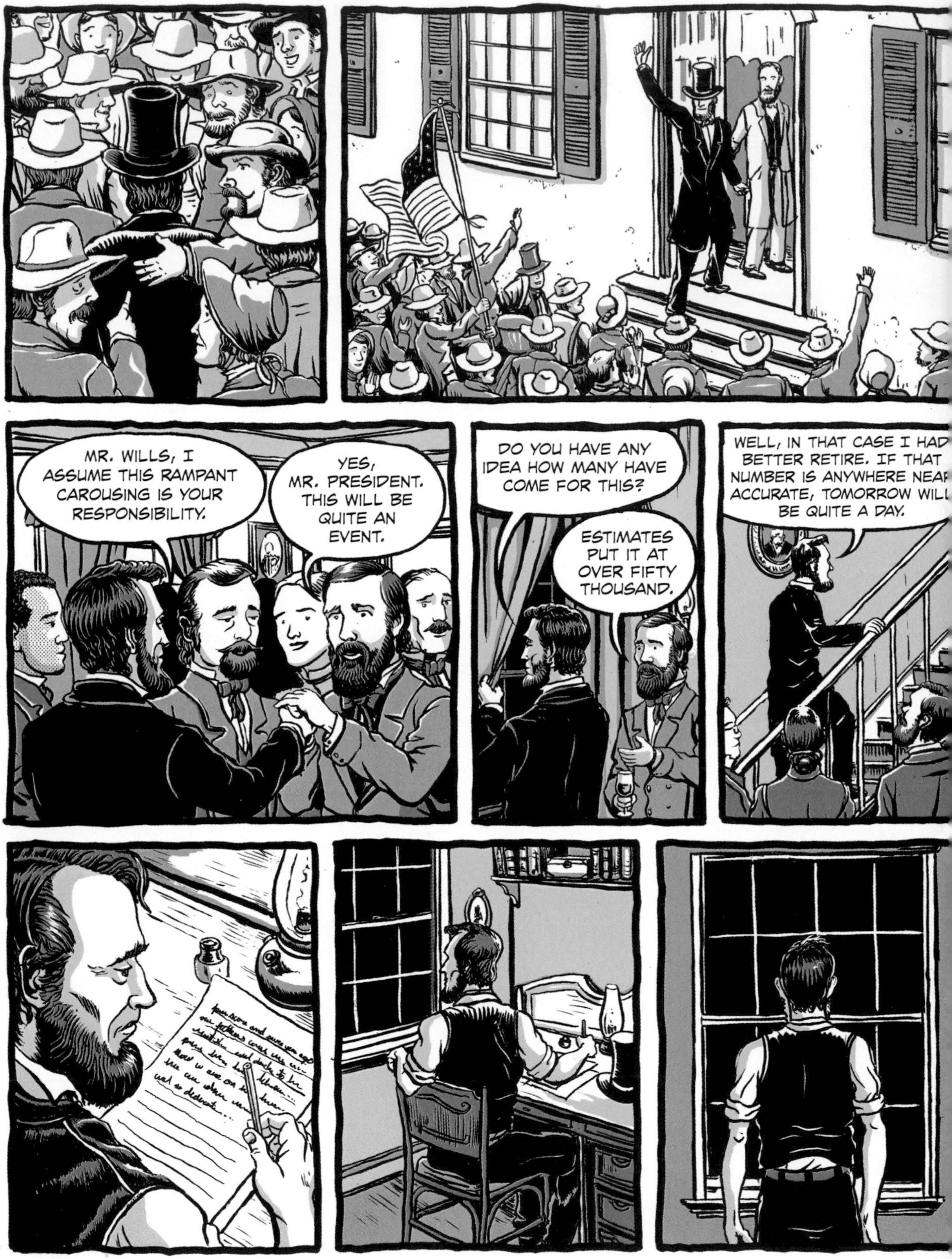
MR. WILLS, I ASSUME THIS RAMPANT CAROUSING IS YOUR RESPONSIBILITY.
YES, MR. PRESIDENT. THIS WILL BE QUITE AN EVENT.
DO YOU HAVE ANY IDEA HOW MANY HAVE COME FOR THIS?
ESTIMATES PUT IT AT OVER FIFTY THOUSAND.
WELL, IN THAT CASE I HAD BETTER RETIRE. IF THAT NUMBER IS ANYWHERE NEAR ACCURATE, TOMORROW WILL BE QUITE A DAY.

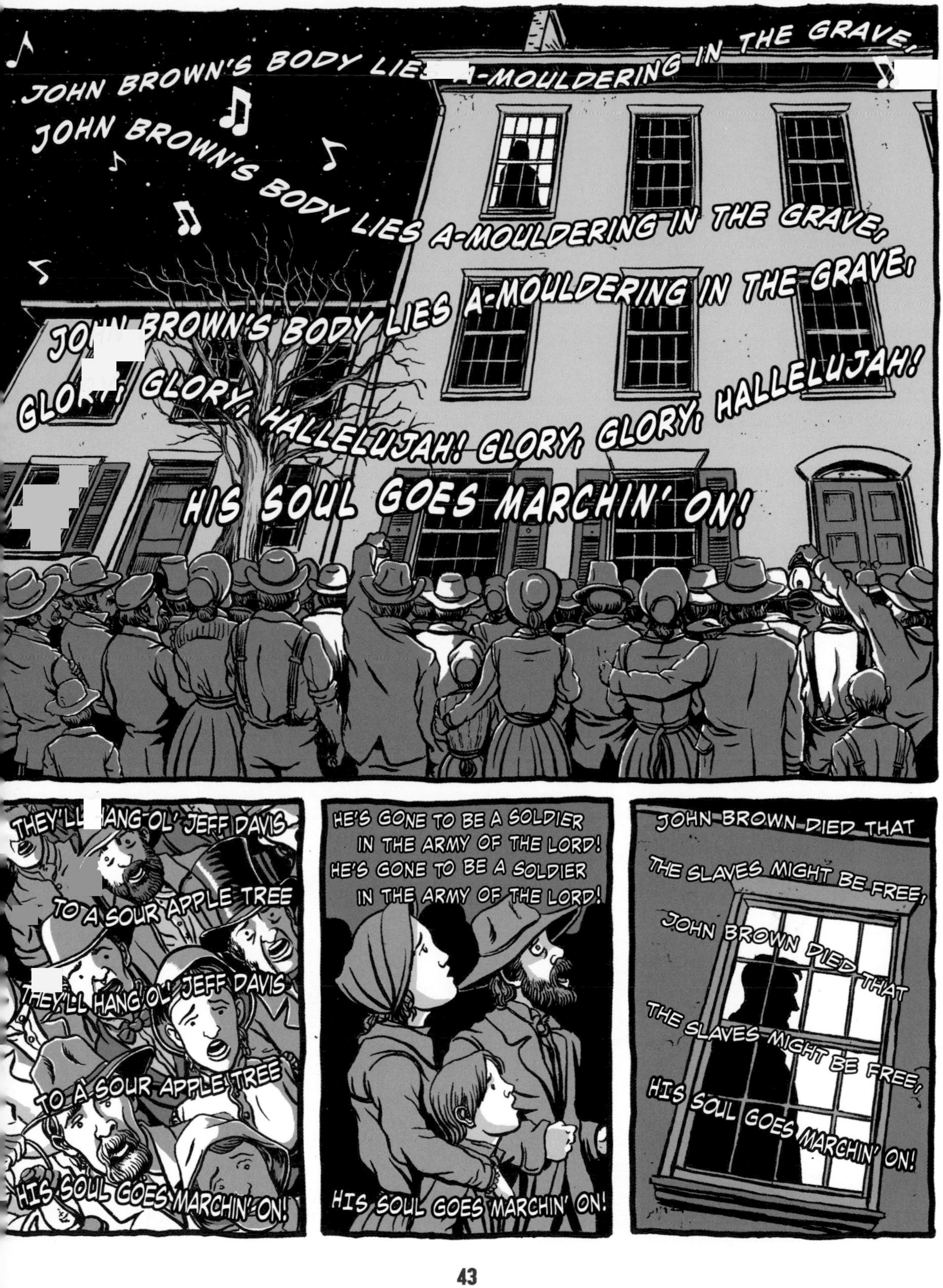

JOHN BROWN'S BODY LIES A-MOULDERING IN THE GRAVE,
JOHN BROWN'S BODY LIES A-MOULDERING IN THE GRAVE,
BROWN'S BODY LIES A-MOULDERING IN THE GRAVE!
GLORY, HALLELUJAH! GLORY, GLORY, HALLELUJAH!
HIS SOUL GOES MARCHIN' ON!
THEY'LL HANG OL' JEFF DAVIS
TO A SOUR APPLE TREE
HANG OL' JEFF DAVIS
TO A SOUR APPLE TREE
HIS SOUL GOES MARCHIN' ON!
HE'S GONE TO BE A SOLDIER IN THE ARMY OF THE LORD!
HE'S GONE TO BE A SOLDIER IN THE ARMY OF THE LORD!
HIS SOUL GOES MARCHIN' ON!
JOHN BROWN DIED THAT
THE SLAVES MIGHT BE FREE,
JOHN BROWN DIED THAT
THE SLAVES MIGHT BE FREE,
HIS SOUL GOES MARCHIN' ON!

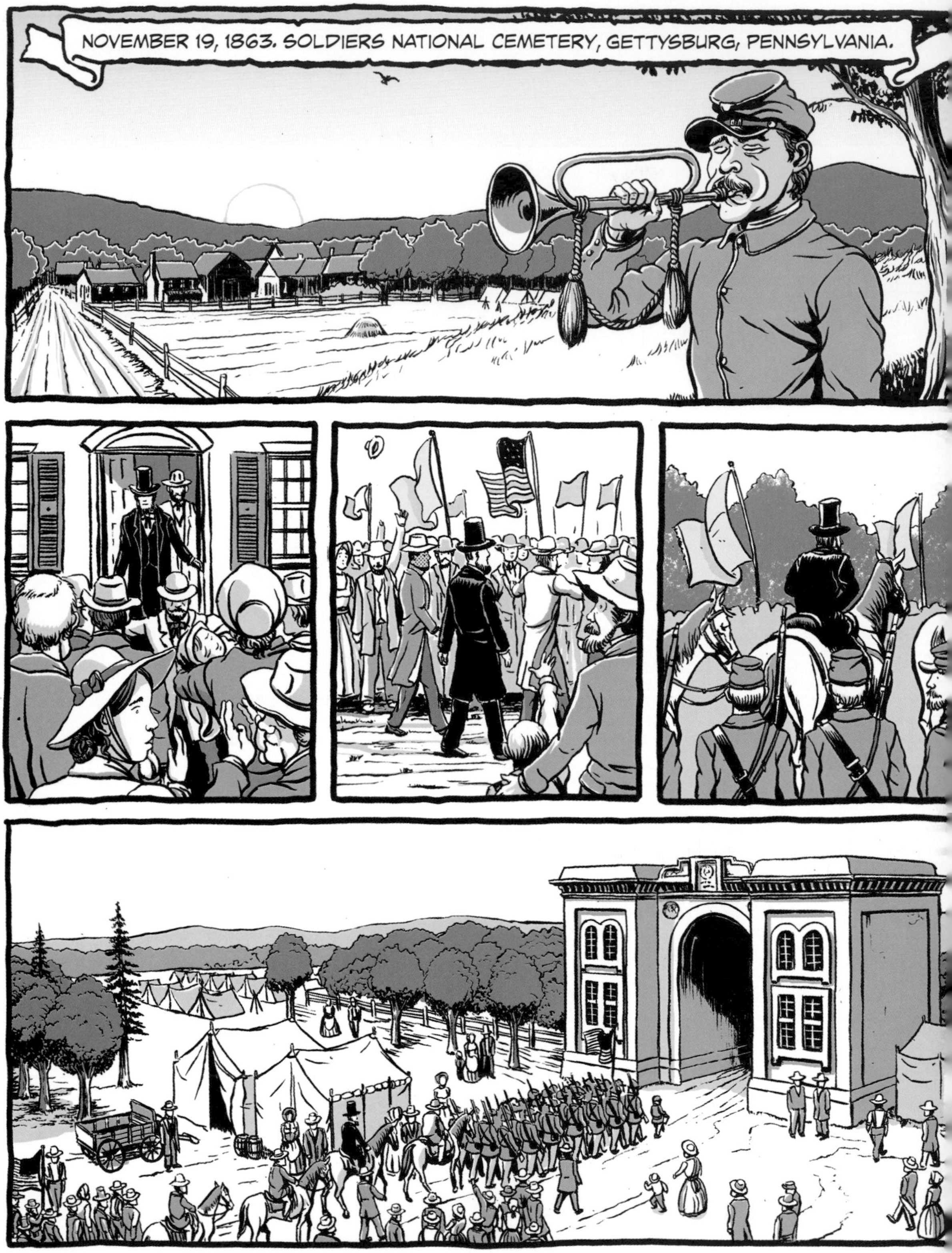
NOVEMBER 19, 1863. SOLDIERS NATIONAL CEMETERY, GETTYSBURG, PENNSYLVANIA.

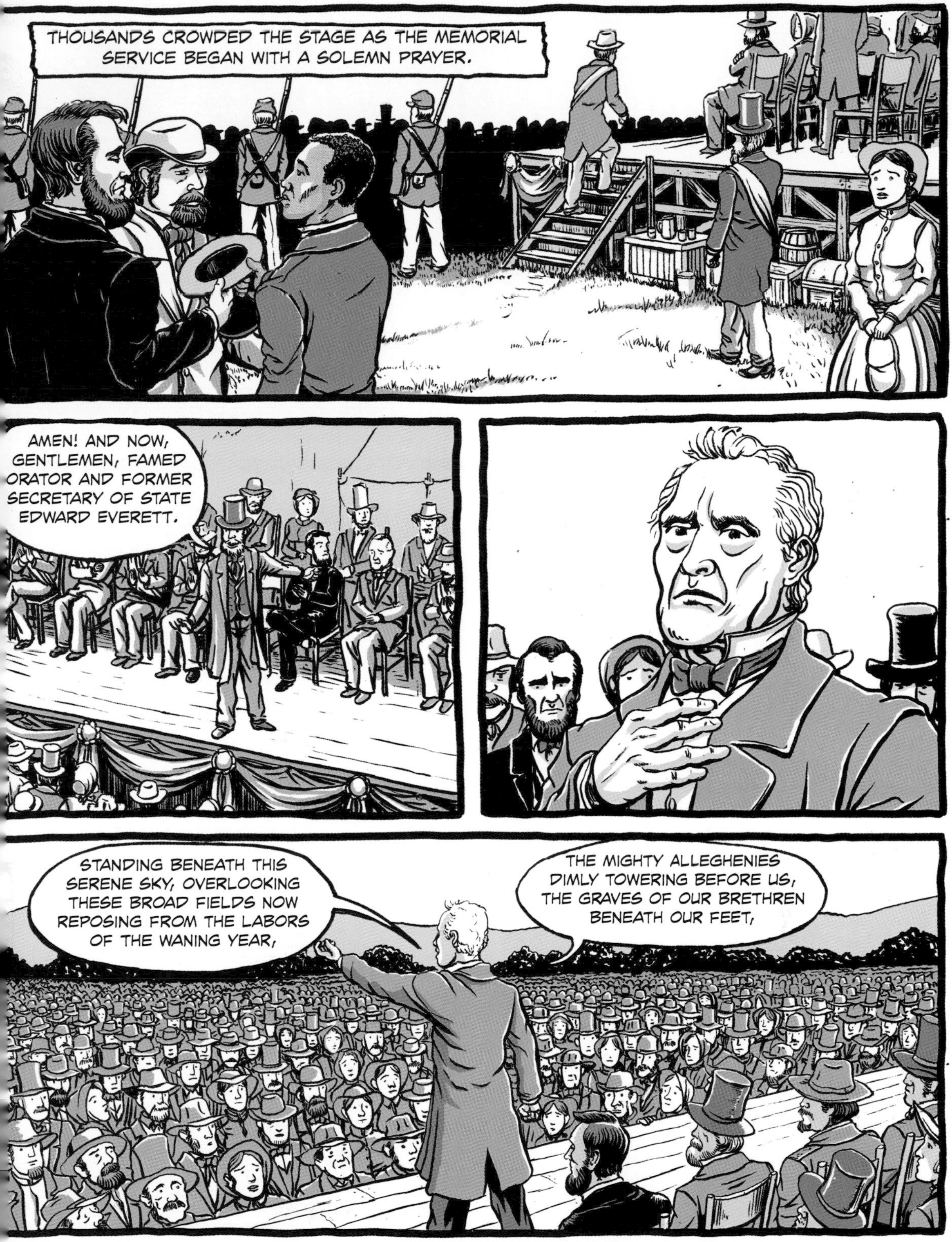

THOUSANDS CROWDED THE STAGE AS THE MEMORIAL SERVICE BEGAN WITH A SOLEMN PRAYER.
AMEN! AND NOW, GENTLEMEN, FAMED ORATOR AND FORMER SECRETARY OF STATE EDWARD EVERETT.
STANDING BENEATH THIS SERENE SKY, OVERLOOKING THESE BROAD FIELDS NOW REPOSING FROM THE LABORS OF THE WANING YEAR,
THE MIGHTY ALLEGHENIES DIMLY TOWERING BEFORE US, THE GRAVES OF OUR BRETHREN BENEATH OUR FEET,

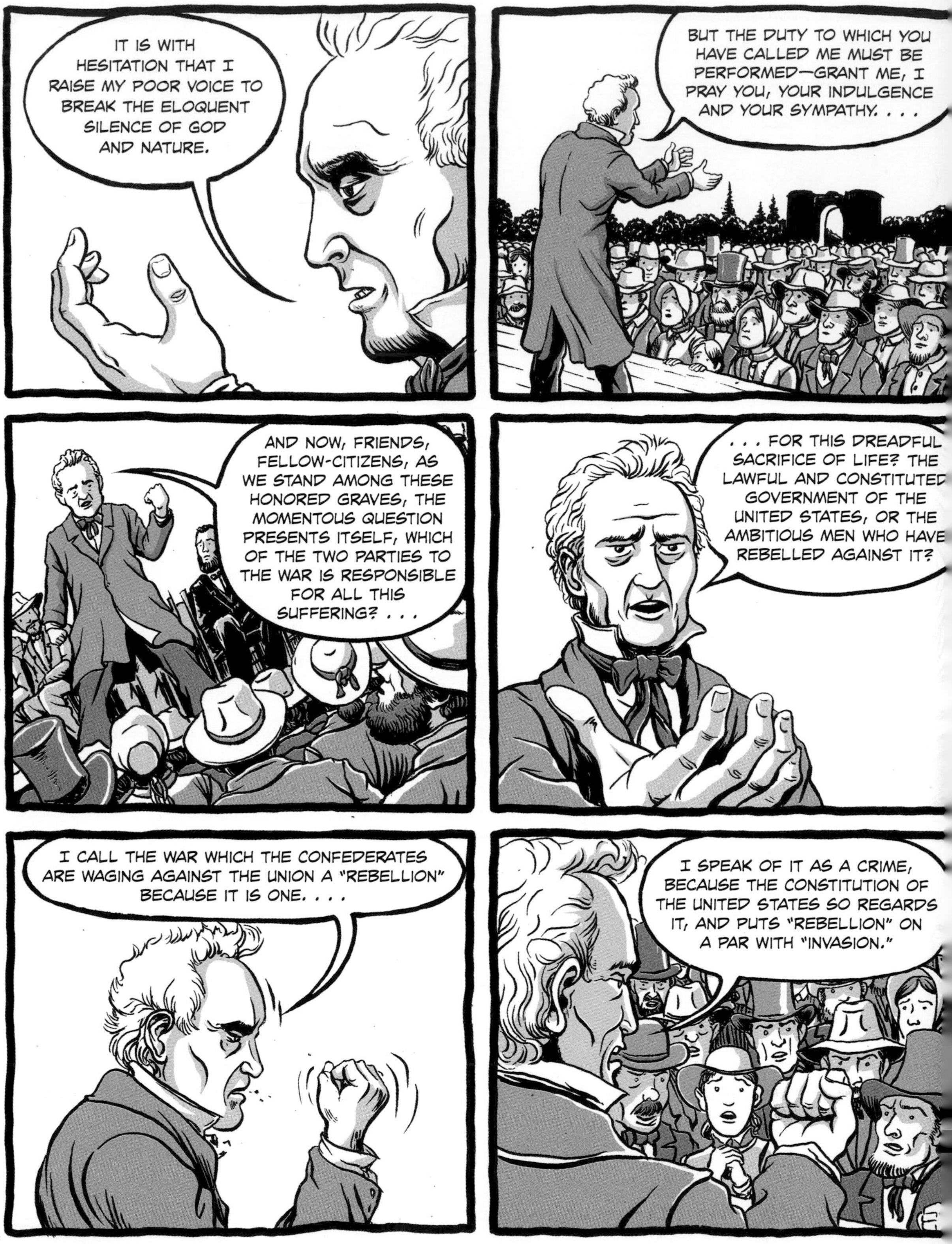
IT IS WITH HESITATION THAT I RAISE MY POOR VOICE TO BREAK THE ELOQUENT SILENCE OF GOD AND NATURE.
BUT THE DUTY TO WHICH YOU HAVE CALLED ME MUST BE PERFORMED—GRANT ME, I PRAY YOU, YOUR INDULGENCE AND YOUR SYMPATHY. . . .
AND NOW, FRIENDS, FELLOW-CITIZENS, AS WE STAND AMONG THESE HONORED GRAVES, THE MOMENTOUS QUESTION PRESENTS ITSELF, WHICH OF THE TWO PARTIES TO THE WAR IS RESPONSIBLE FOR ALL THIS SUFFERING? . . .
. . . FOR THIS DREADFUL SACRIFICE OF LIFE? THE LAWFUL AND CONSTITUTED GOVERNMENT OF THE UNITED STATES, OR THE AMBITIOUS MEN WHO HAVE REBELLED AGAINST IT?
I CALL THE WAR WHICH THE CONFEDERATES ARE WAGING AGAINST THE UNION A "REBELLION" BECAUSE IT IS ONE. . . .
I SPEAK OF IT AS A CRIME, BECAUSE THE CONSTITUTION OF THE UNITED STATES SO REGARDS IT, AND PUTS "REBELLION" ON A PAR WITH "INVASION."

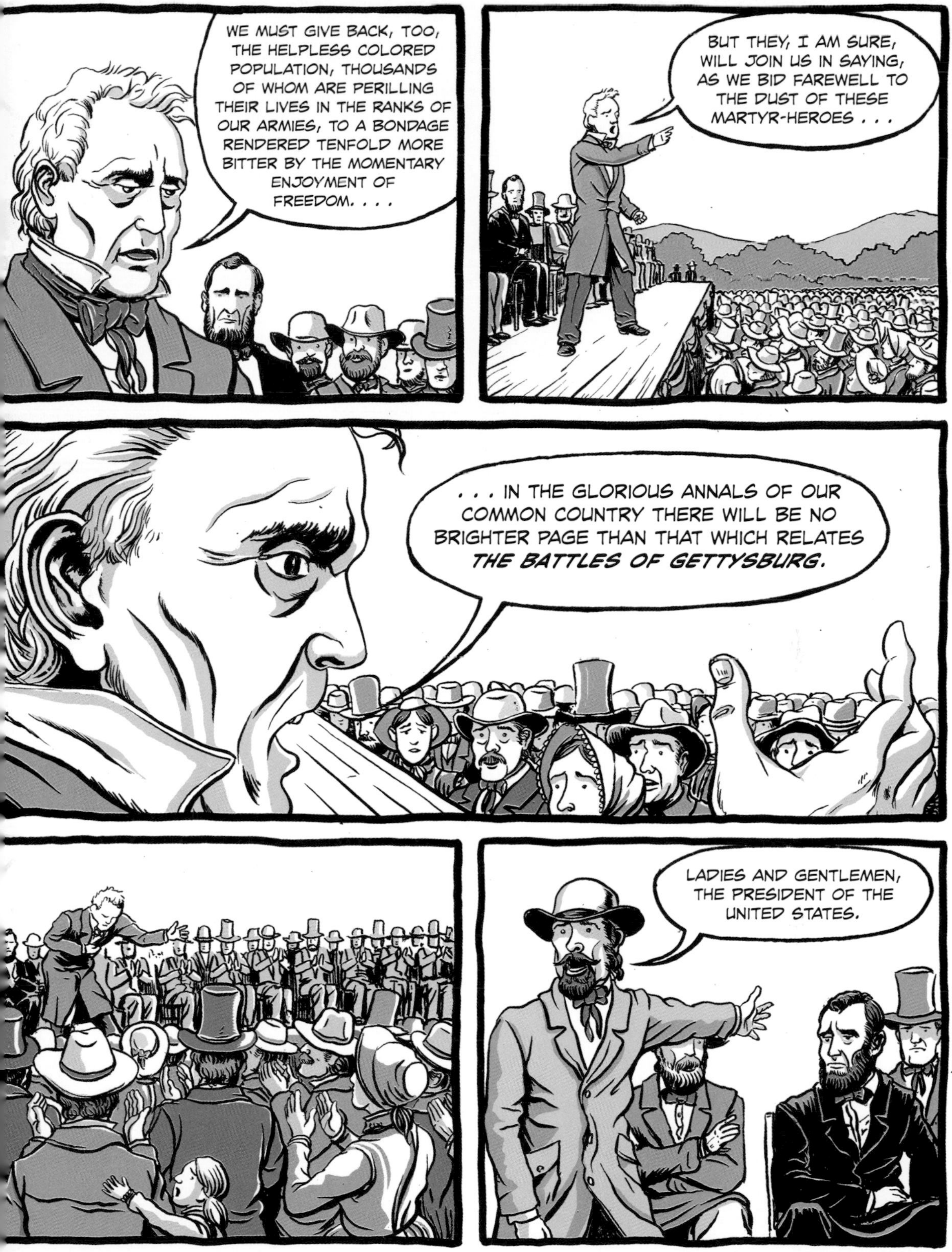
WE MUST GIVE BACK, TOO, THE HELPLESS COLORED POPULATION, THOUSANDS OF WHOM ARE PERILLING THEIR LIVES IN THE RANKS OF OUR ARMIES, TO A BONDAGE RENDERED TENFOLD MORE BITTER BY THE MOMENTARY ENJOYMENT OF FREEDOM. . . .
BUT THEY, I AM SURE, WILL JOIN US IN SAYING, AS WE BID FAREWELL TO THE DUST OF THESE MARTYR-HEROES . . .
. . . IN THE GLORIOUS ANNALS OF OUR COMMON COUNTRY THERE WILL BE NO BRIGHTER PAGE THAN THAT WHICH RELATES *THE BATTLES OF GETTYSBURG.*
LADIES AND GENTLEMEN, THE PRESIDENT OF THE UNITED STATES.

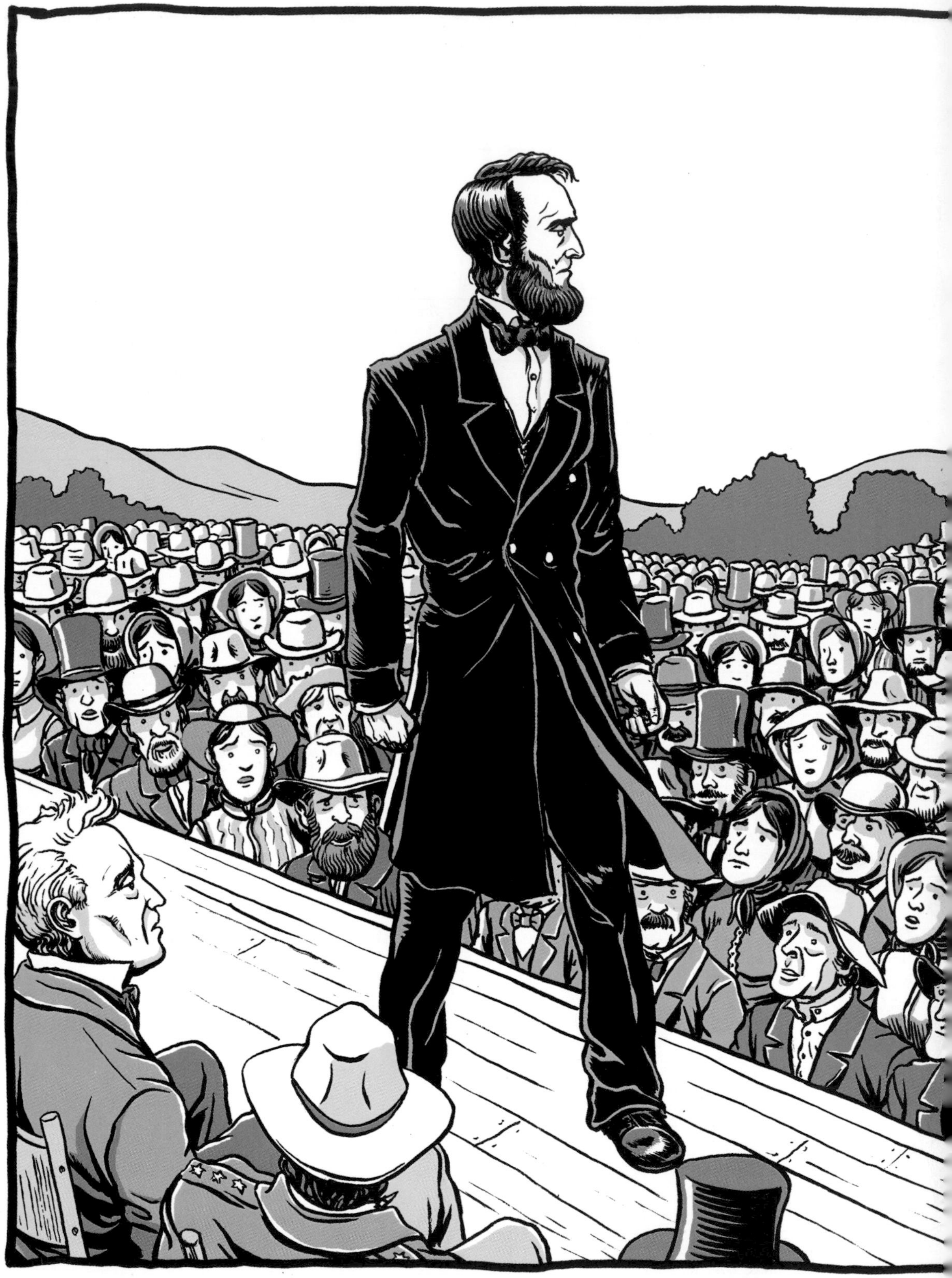

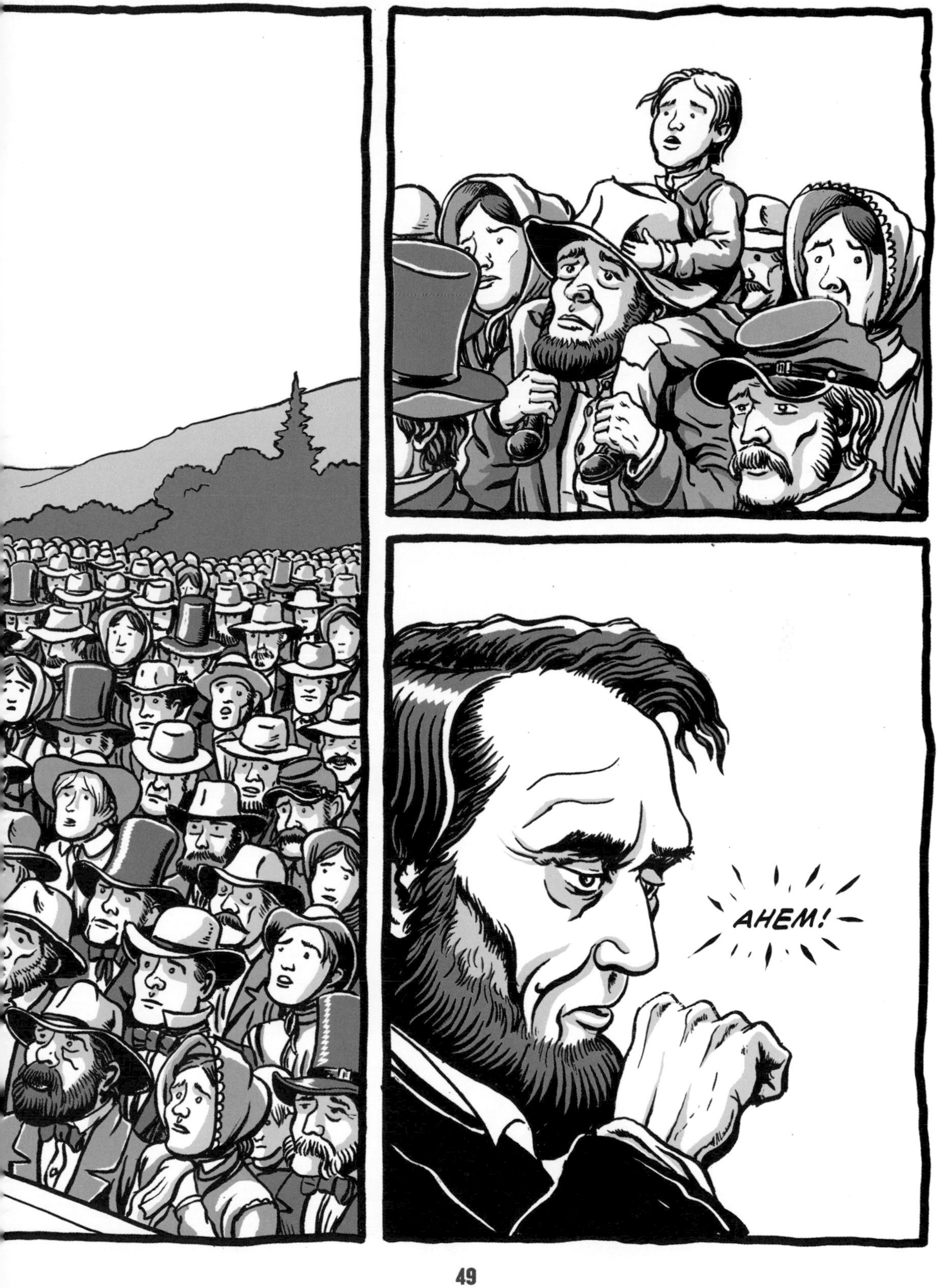
AHEM!

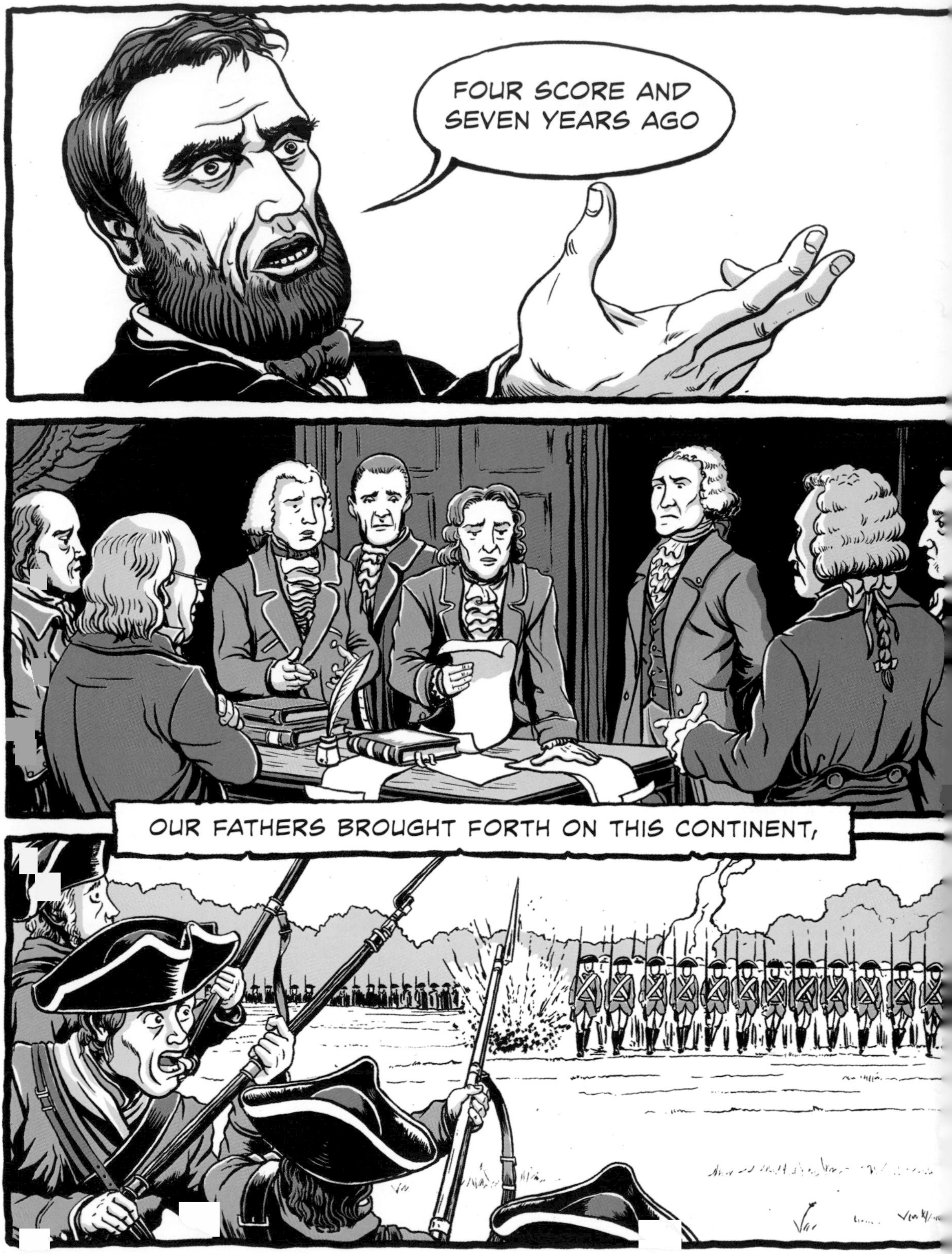
FOUR SCORE AND SEVEN YEARS AGO
OUR FATHERS BROUGHT FORTH ON THIS CONTINENT,

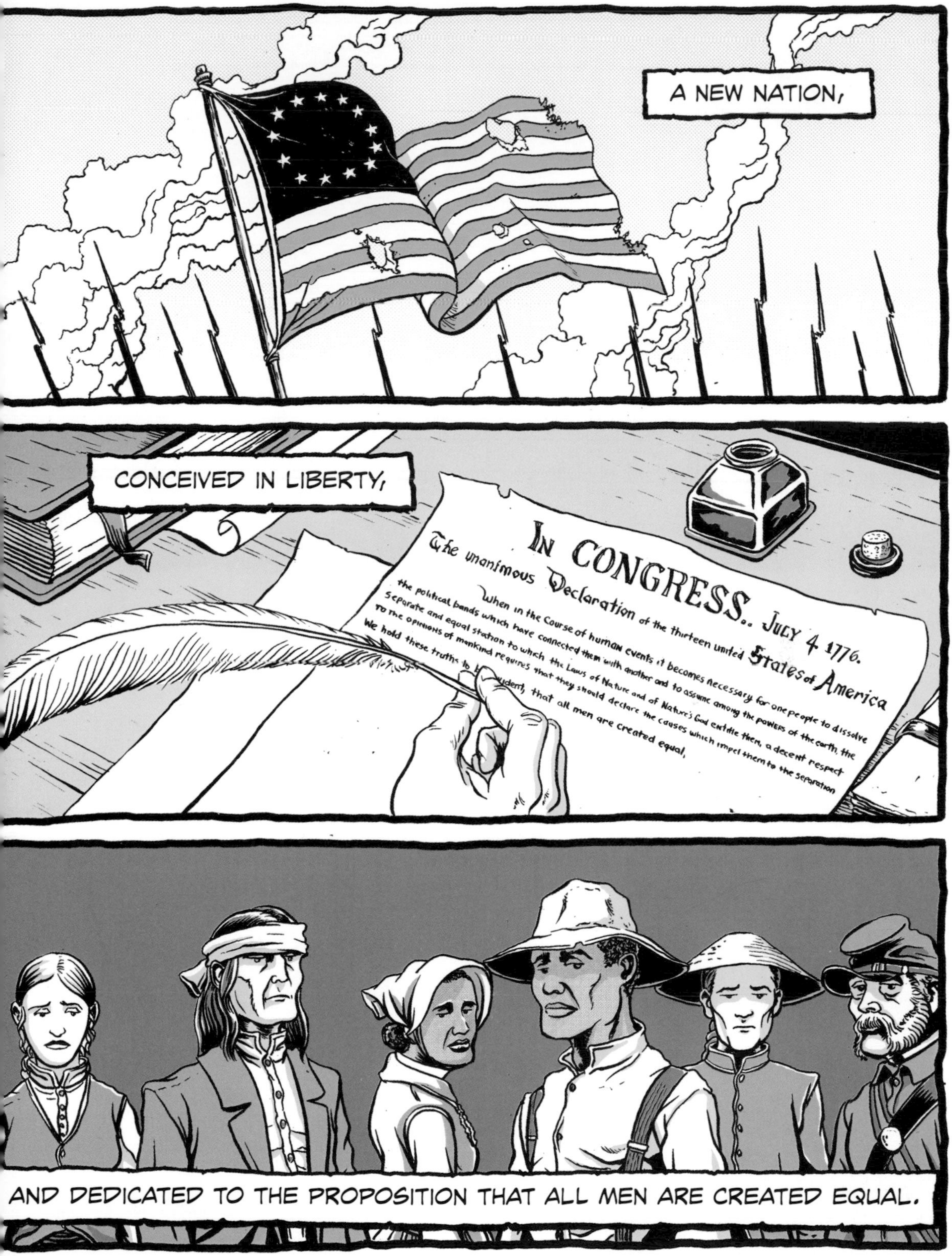
A NEW NATION,
CONCEIVED IN LIBERTY,
IN CONGRESS. JULY 4 1776.
The unanimous Declaration of the thirteen united States of America
When in the Course of human events it becomes necessary for one people to dissolve
the political bands which have connected them with another and to assume among the powers of the earth, the
separate and equal station to which the Laws of Nature and of Nature's God entitle them, a decent respect
to the opinions of mankind requires that they should declare the causes which impel them to the separation
AND DEDICATED TO THE PROPOSITION THAT ALL MEN ARE CREATED EQUAL.

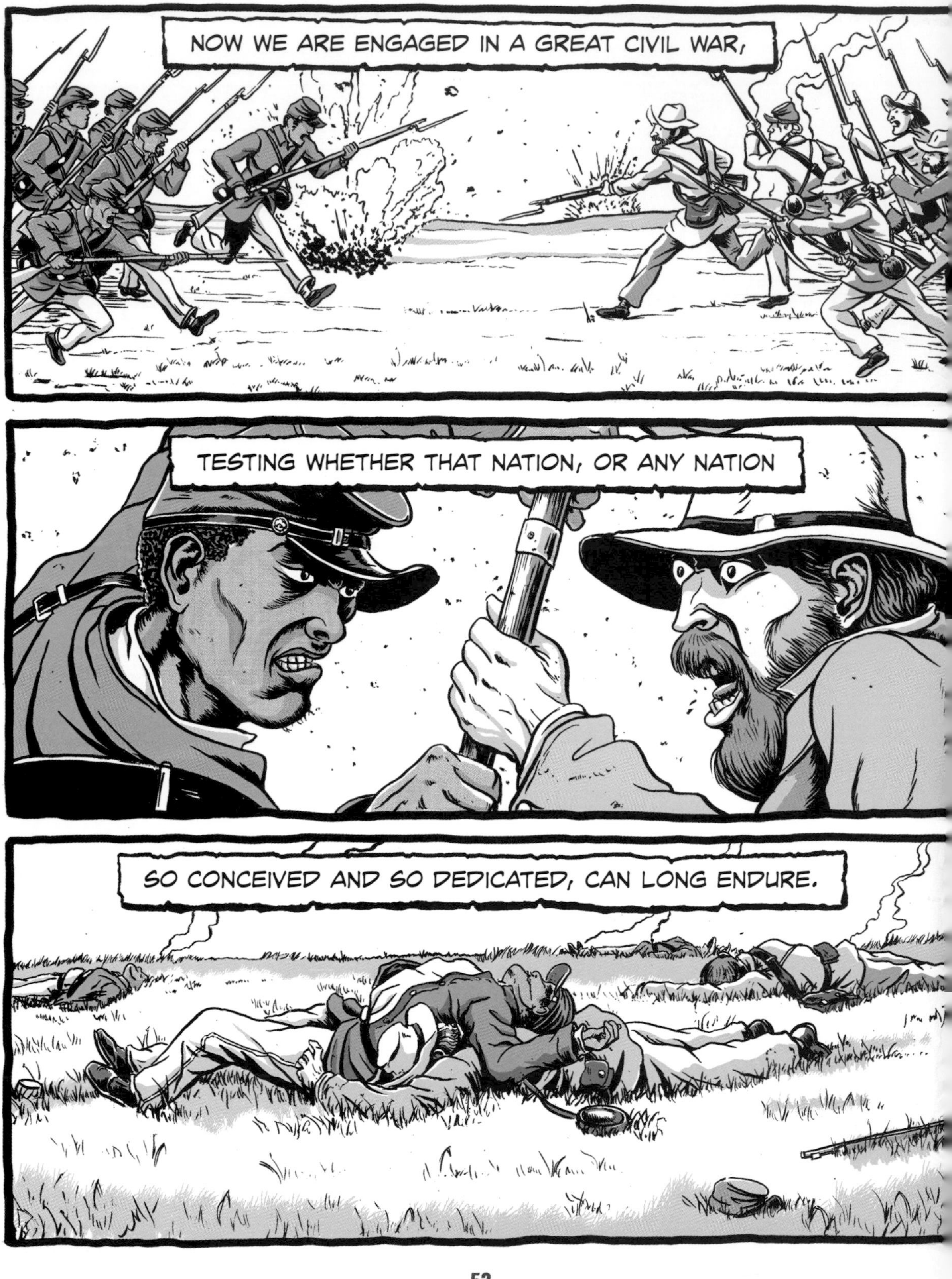
NOW WE ARE ENGAGED IN A GREAT CIVIL WAR,
TESTING WHETHER THAT NATION, OR ANY NATION
SO CONCEIVED AND SO DEDICATED, CAN LONG ENDURE.

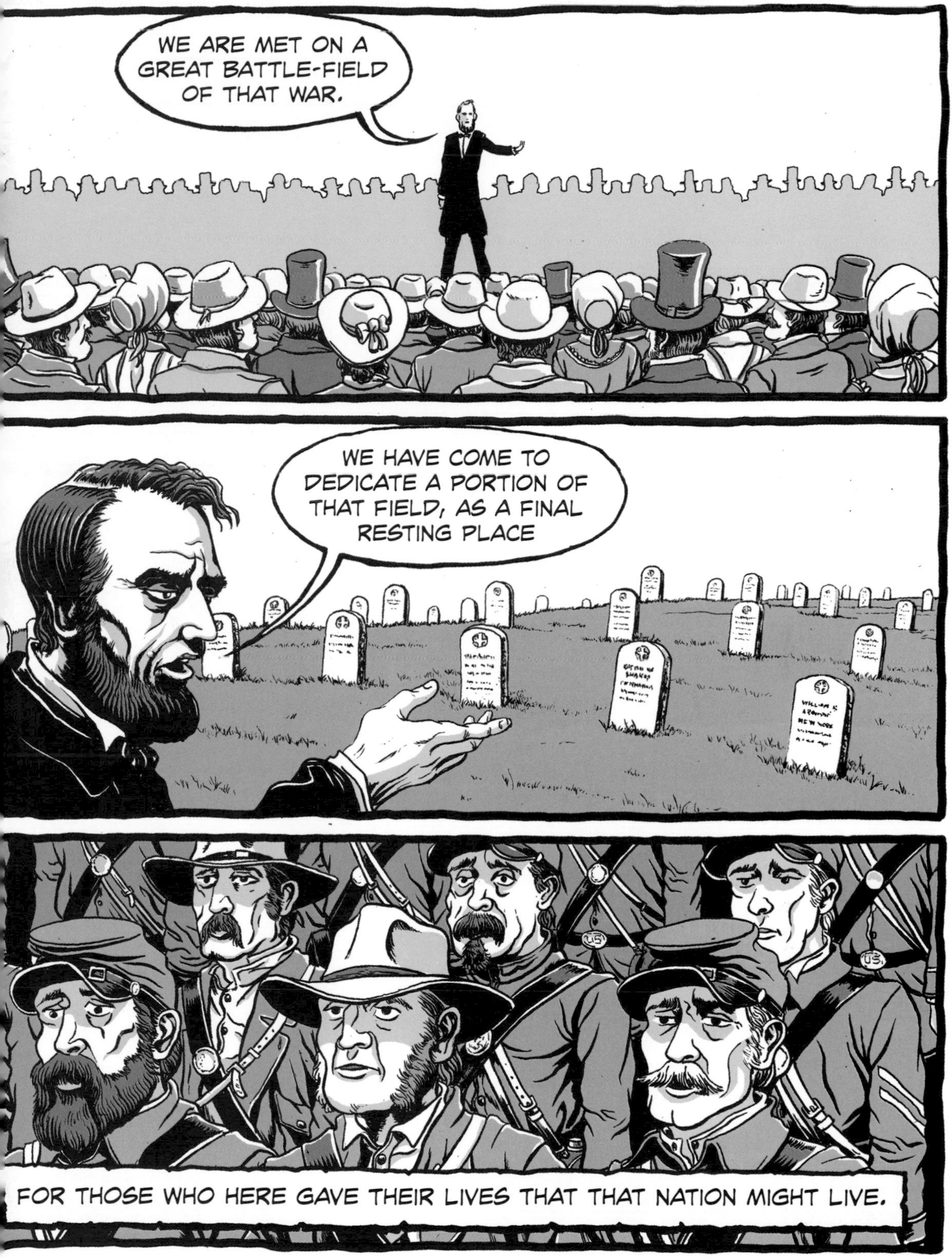
WE ARE MET ON A GREAT BATTLE-FIELD OF THAT WAR.
WE HAVE COME TO DEDICATE A PORTION OF THAT FIELD, AS A FINAL RESTING PLACE
FOR THOSE WHO HERE GAVE THEIR LIVES THAT THAT NATION MIGHT LIVE.

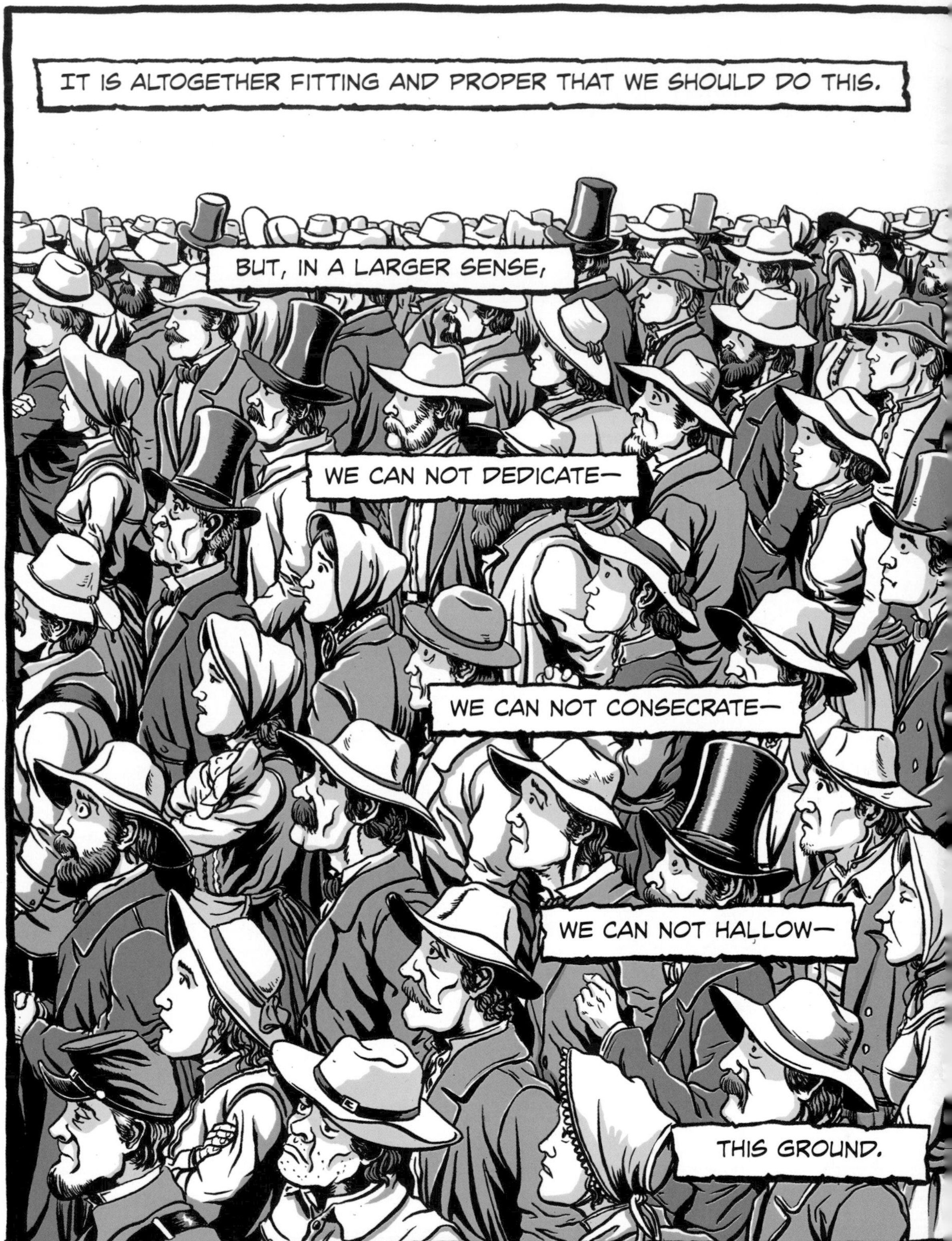
IT IS ALTOGETHER FITTING AND PROPER THAT WE SHOULD DO THIS.
BUT, IN A LARGER SENSE,
WE CAN NOT DEDICATE—
WE CAN NOT CONSECRATE—
WE CAN NOT HALLOW—
THIS GROUND.

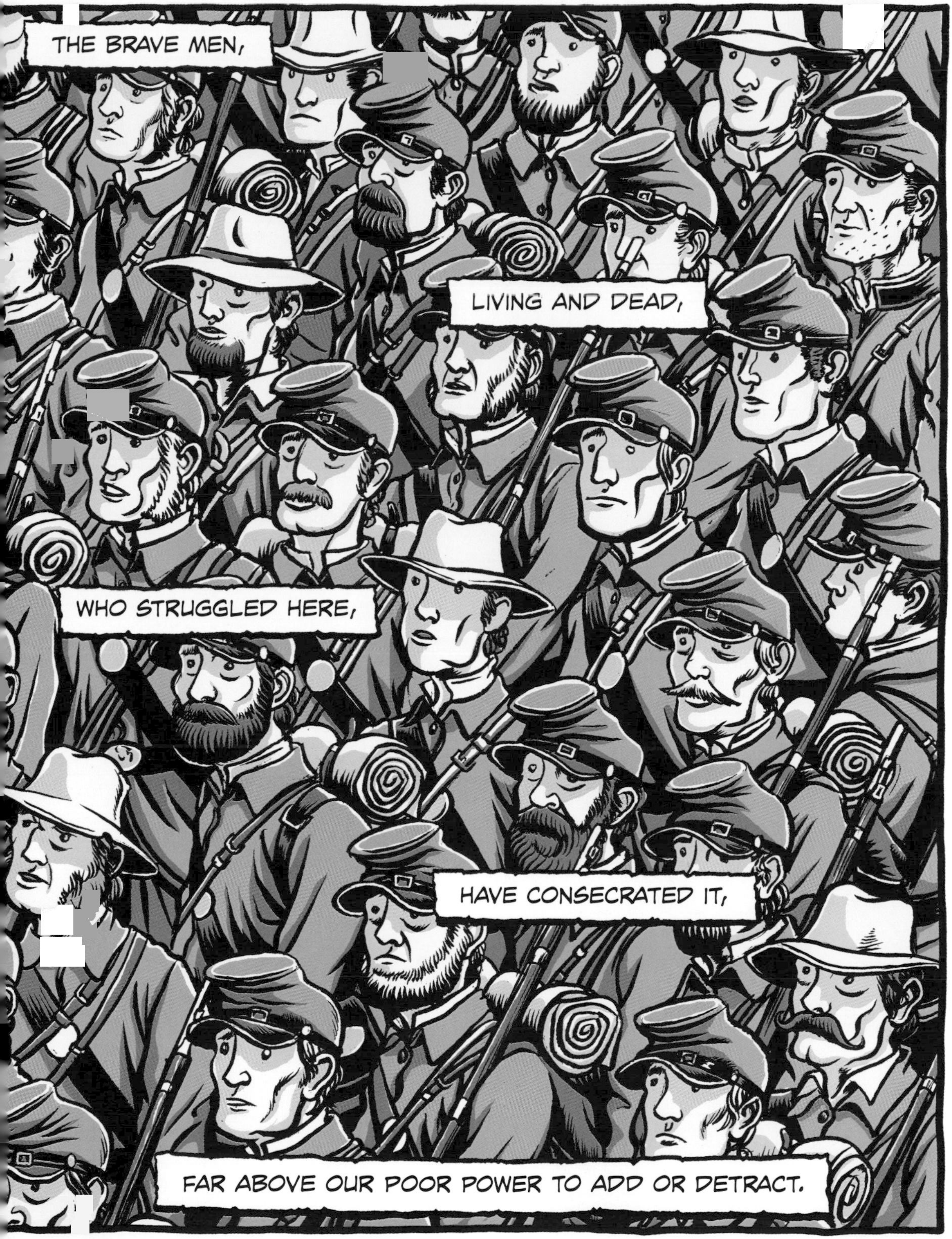
THE BRAVE MEN,
LIVING AND DEAD,
WHO STRUGGLED HERE,
HAVE CONSECRATED IT,
FAR ABOVE OUR POOR POWER TO ADD OR DETRACT.

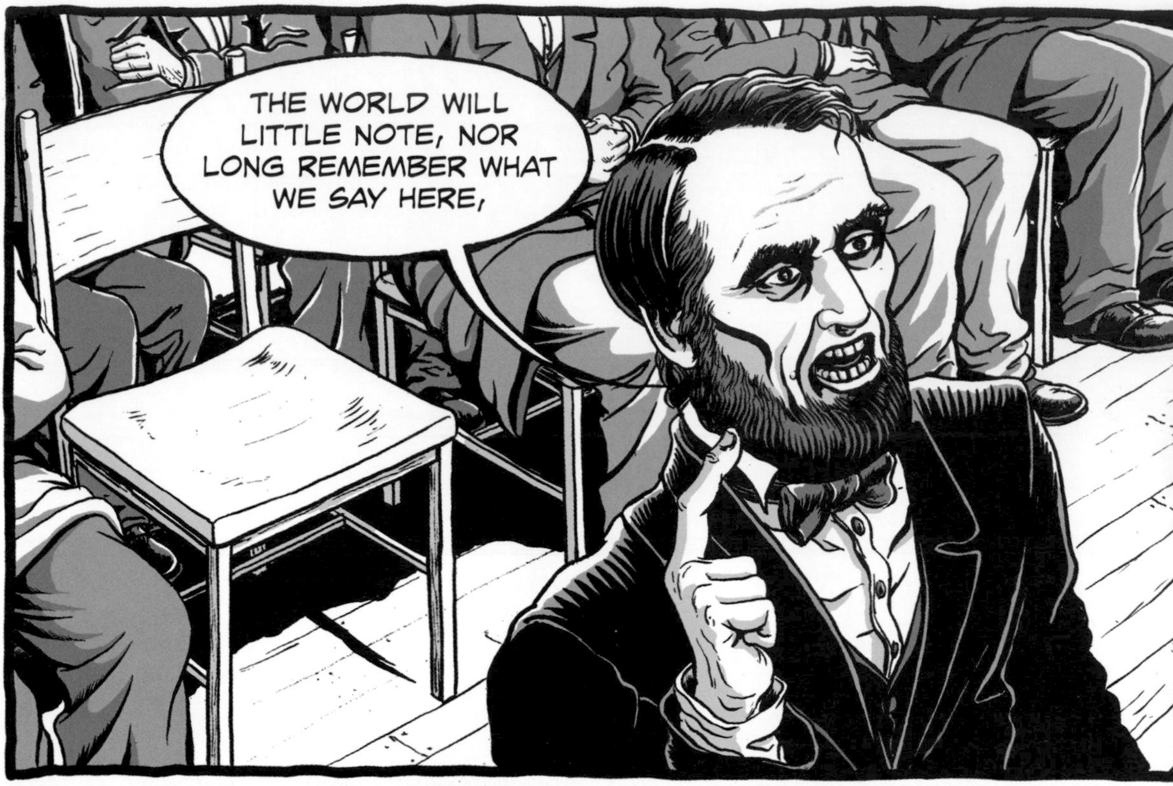
THE WORLD WILL LITTLE NOTE, NOR LONG REMEMBER WHAT WE SAY HERE,

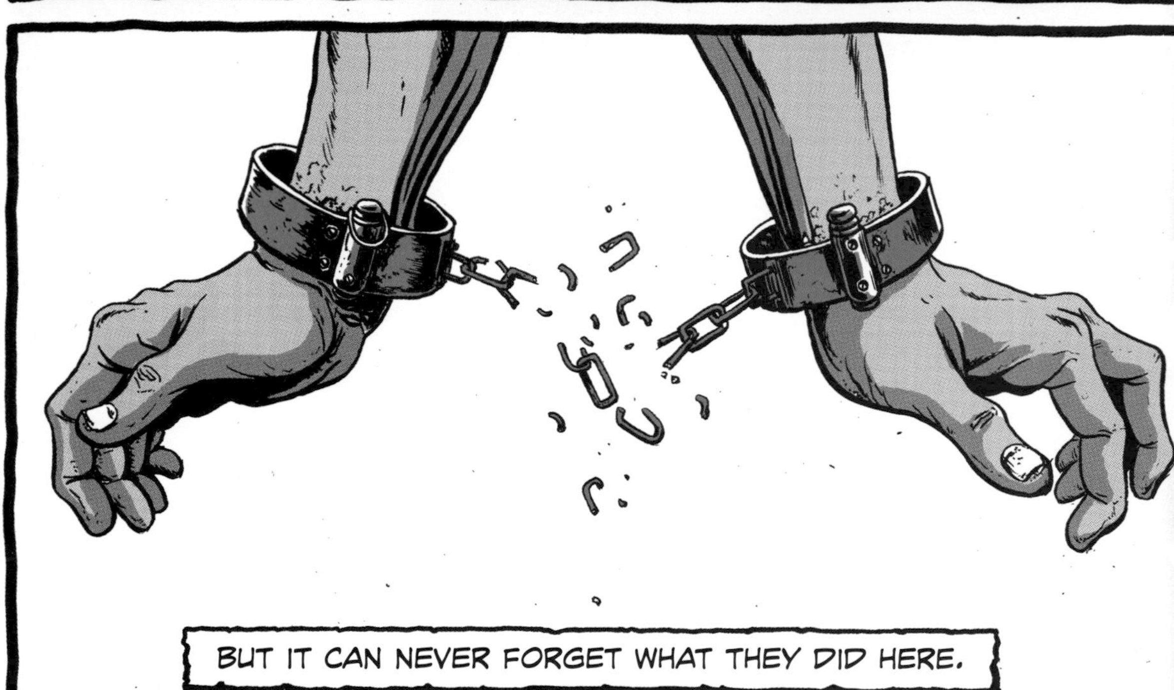
BUT IT CAN NEVER FORGET WHAT THEY DID HERE.

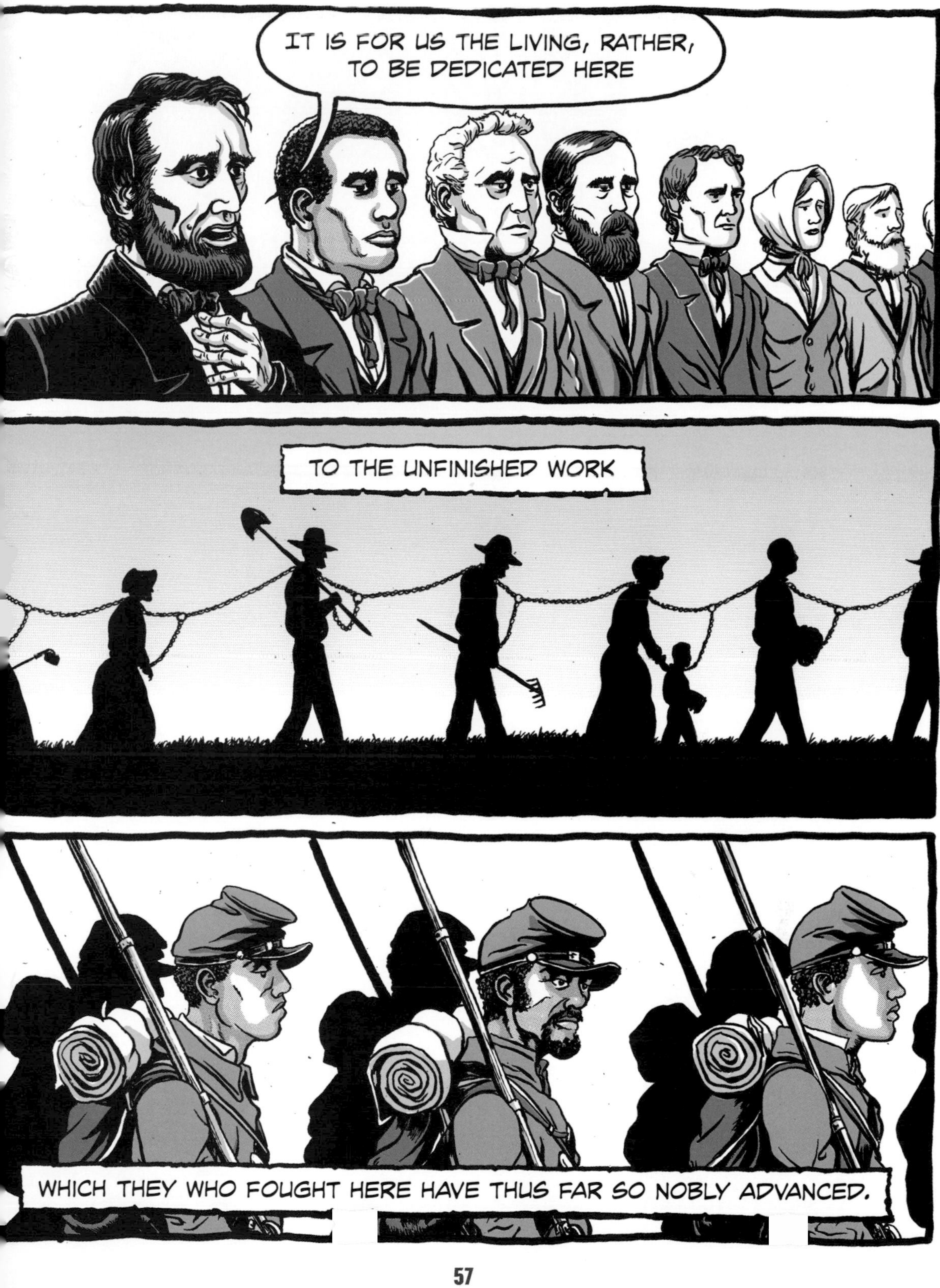
IT IS FOR US THE LIVING, RATHER, TO BE DEDICATED HERE
TO THE UNFINISHED WORK
WHICH THEY WHO FOUGHT HERE HAVE THUS FAR SO NOBLY ADVANCED.

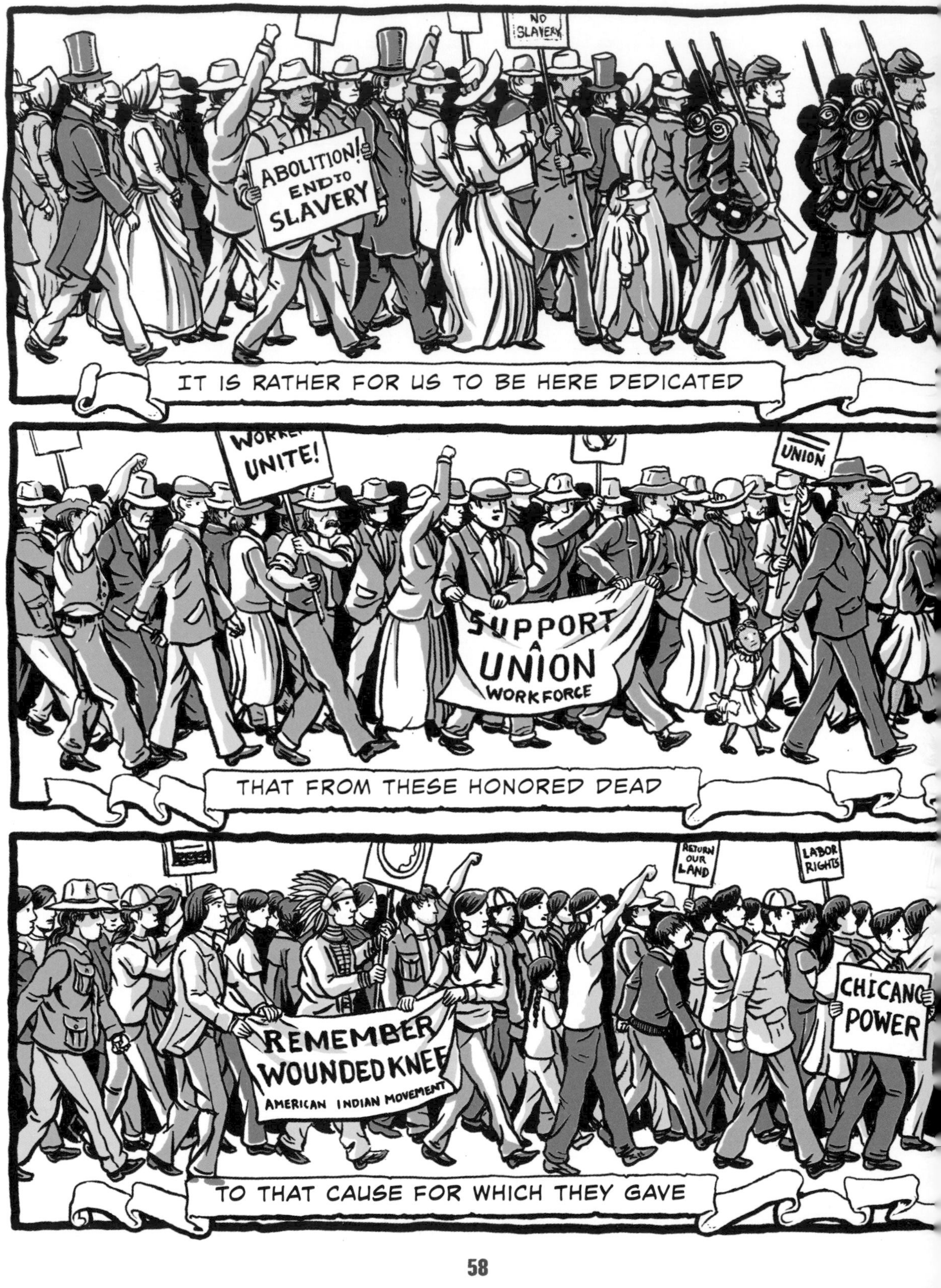
NO SLAVERY
ABOLITION! END TO SLAVERY
IT IS RATHER FOR US TO BE HERE DEDICATED
UNITE!
UNION
SUPPORT A UNION WORKFORCE
THAT FROM THESE HONORED DEAD
RETURN OUR LAND
LABOR RIGHTS
REMEMBER WOUNDED KNEE
AMERICAN INDIAN MOVEMENT
CHICANO POWER
TO THAT CAUSE FOR WHICH THEY GAVE

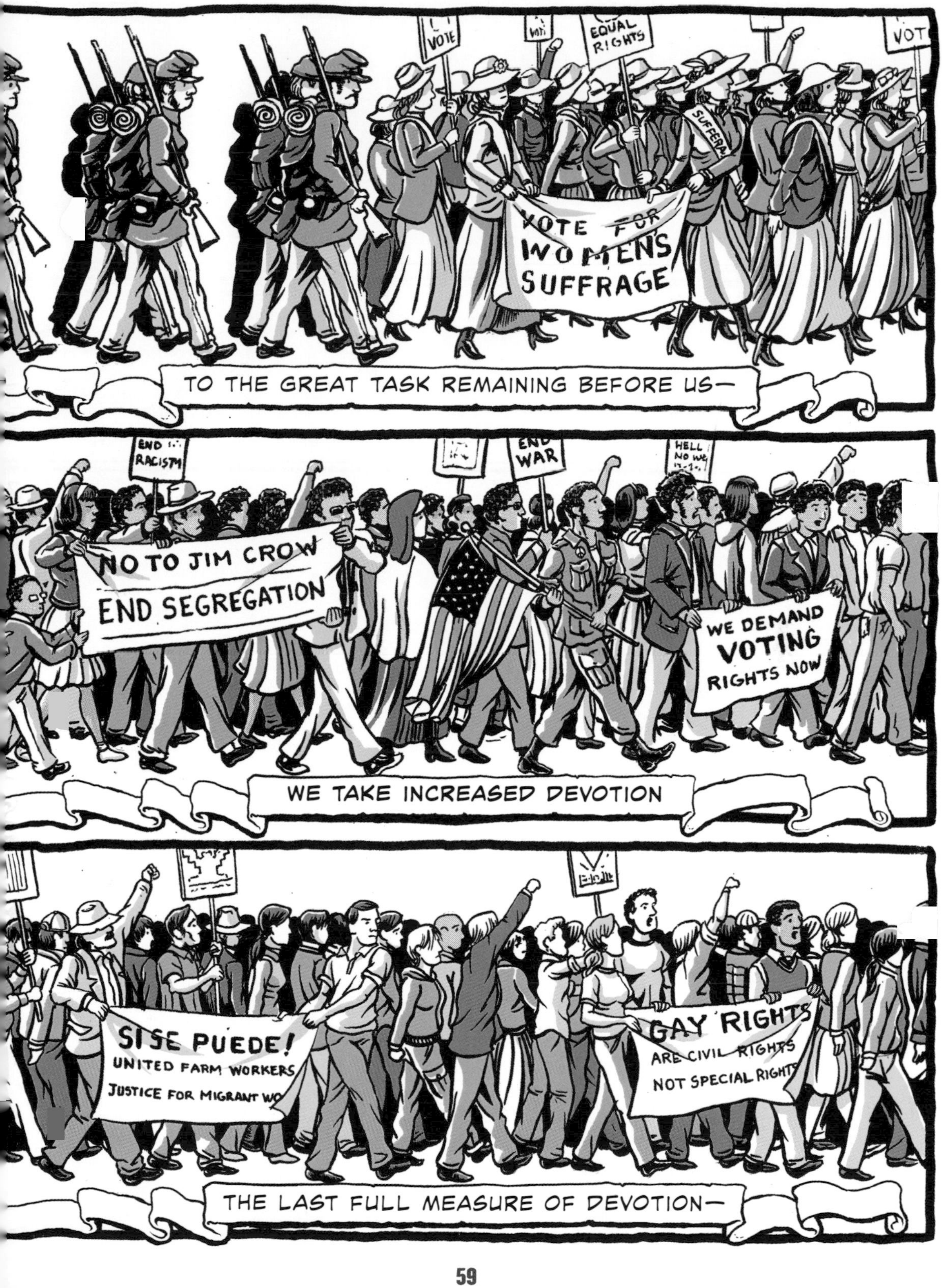
VOTE
EQUAL RIGHTS
VOTE FOR WOMENS SUFFRAGE
TO THE GREAT TASK REMAINING BEFORE US—
END WAR
NO TO JIM CROW
END SEGREGATION
WE DEMAND VOTING RIGHTS NOW
WE TAKE INCREASED DEVOTION
SI SE PUEDE!
UNITED FARM WORKERS
GAY RIGHTS
ARE CIVIL RIGHTS
NOT SPECIAL RIGHTS
THE LAST FULL MEASURE OF DEVOTION—

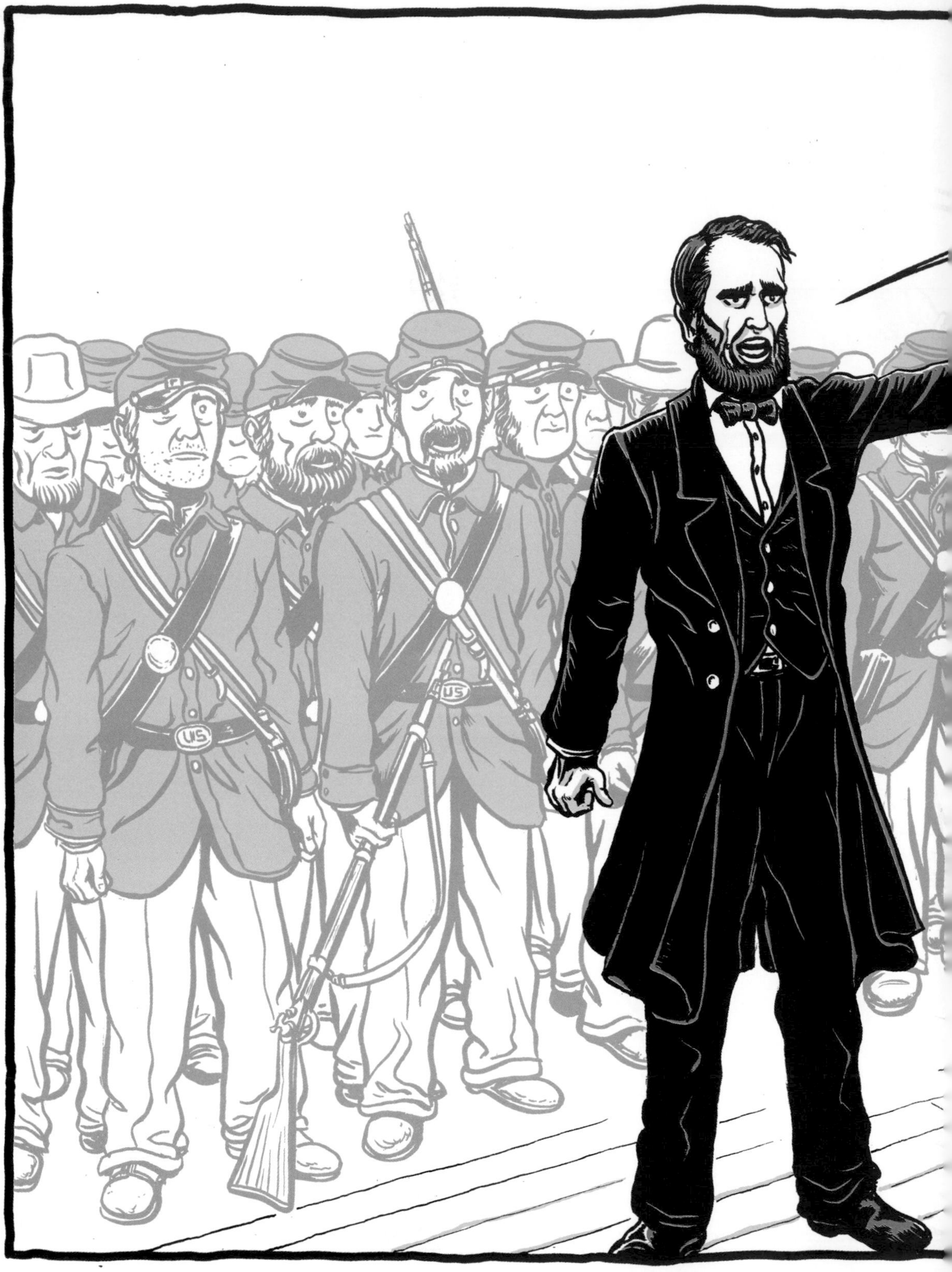
US
US
US

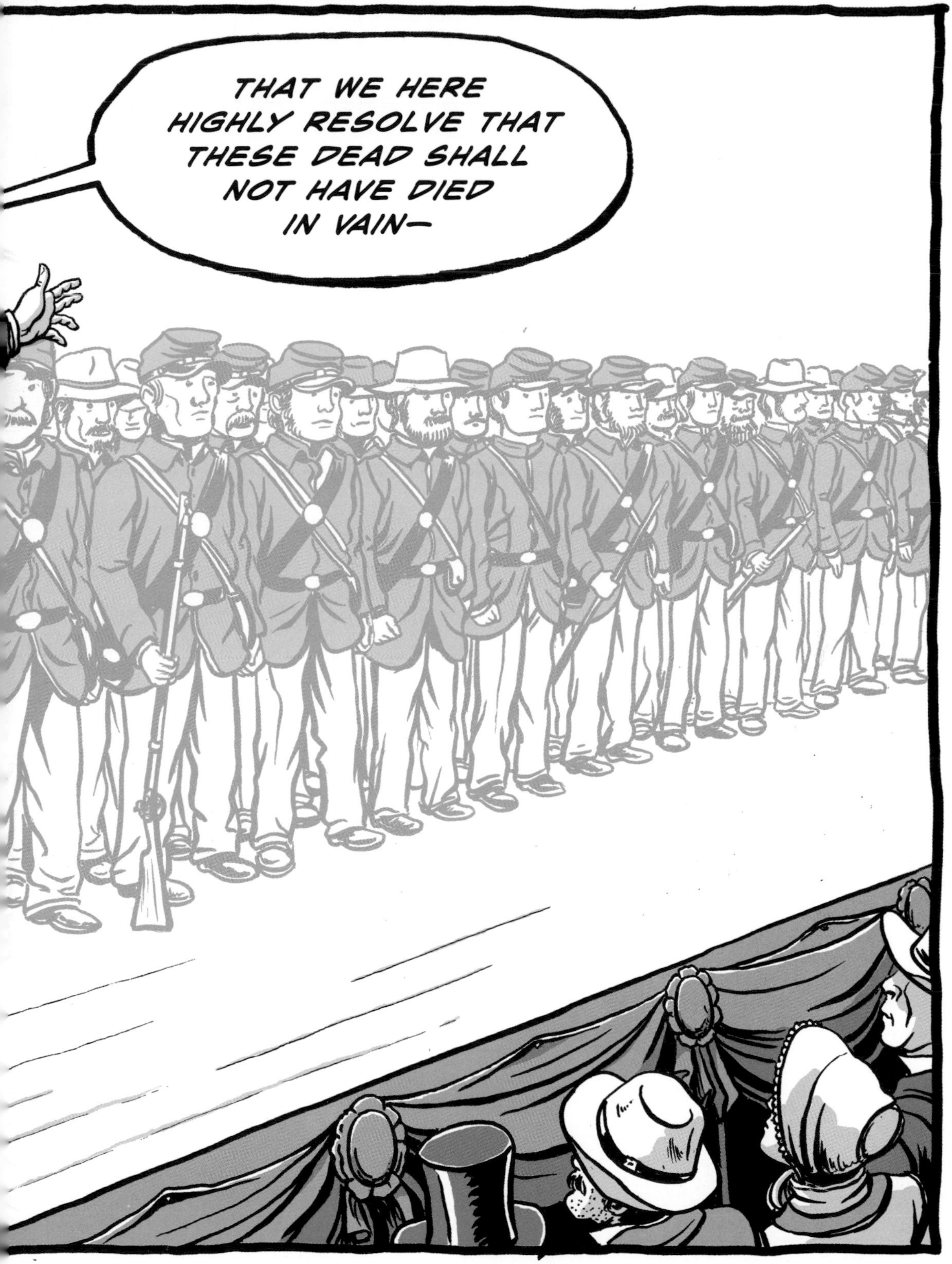
THAT WE HERE HIGHLY RESOLVE THAT THESE DEAD SHALL NOT HAVE DIED IN VAIN—

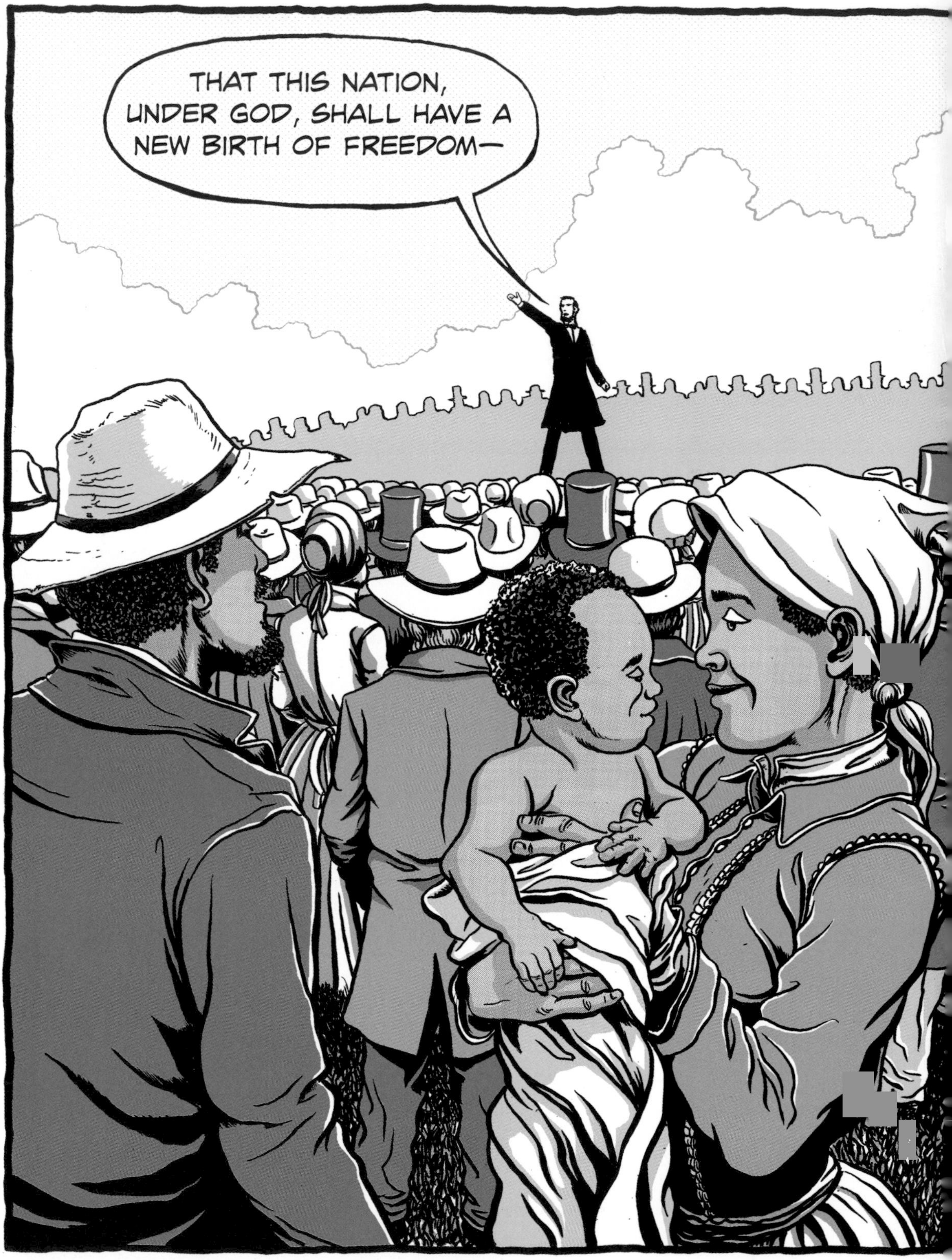
THAT THIS NATION, UNDER GOD, SHALL HAVE A NEW BIRTH OF FREEDOM—

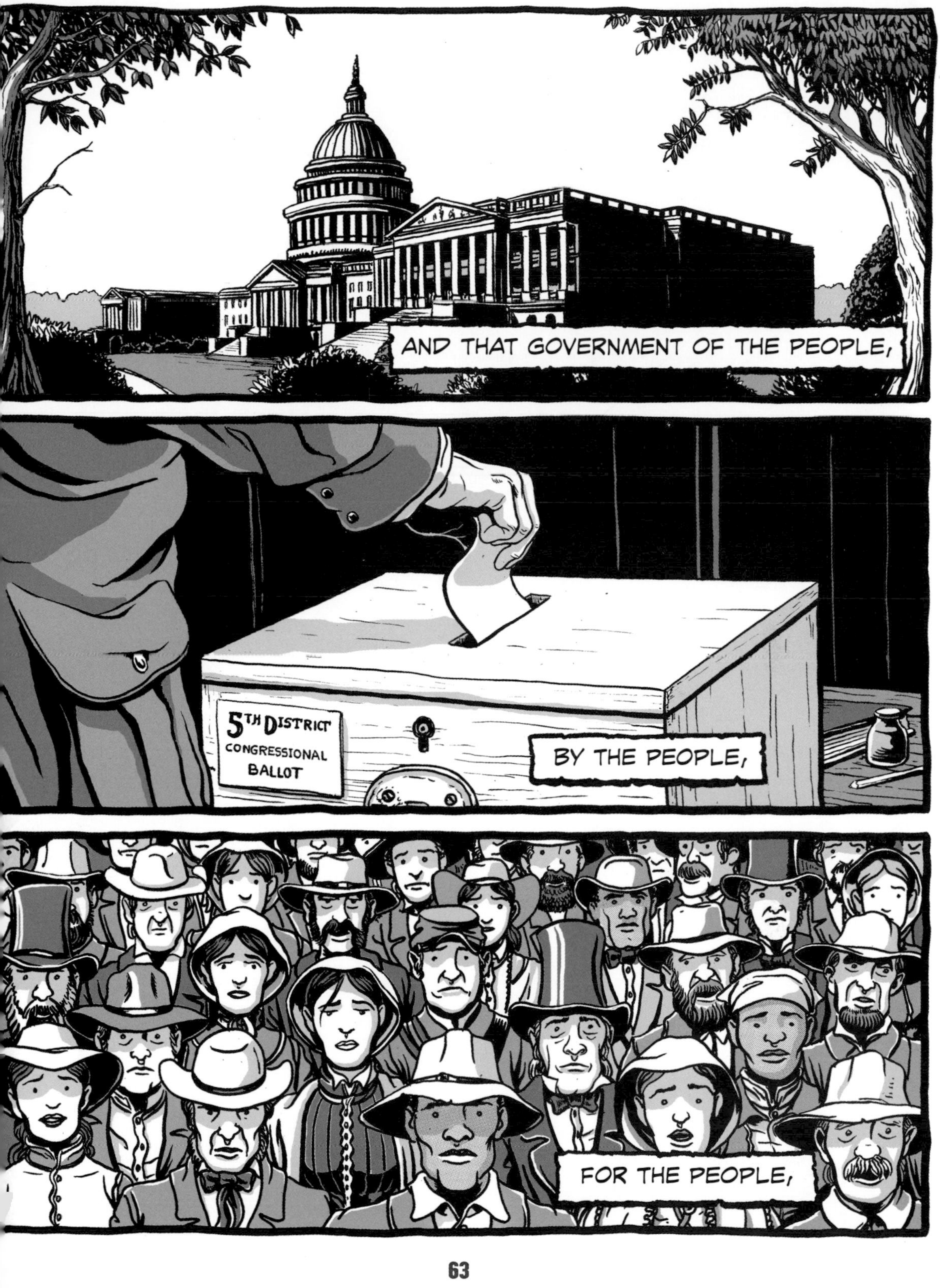
AND THAT GOVERNMENT OF THE PEOPLE,
5TH DISTRICT
CONGRESSIONAL
BALLOT
BY THE PEOPLE,
FOR THE PEOPLE,

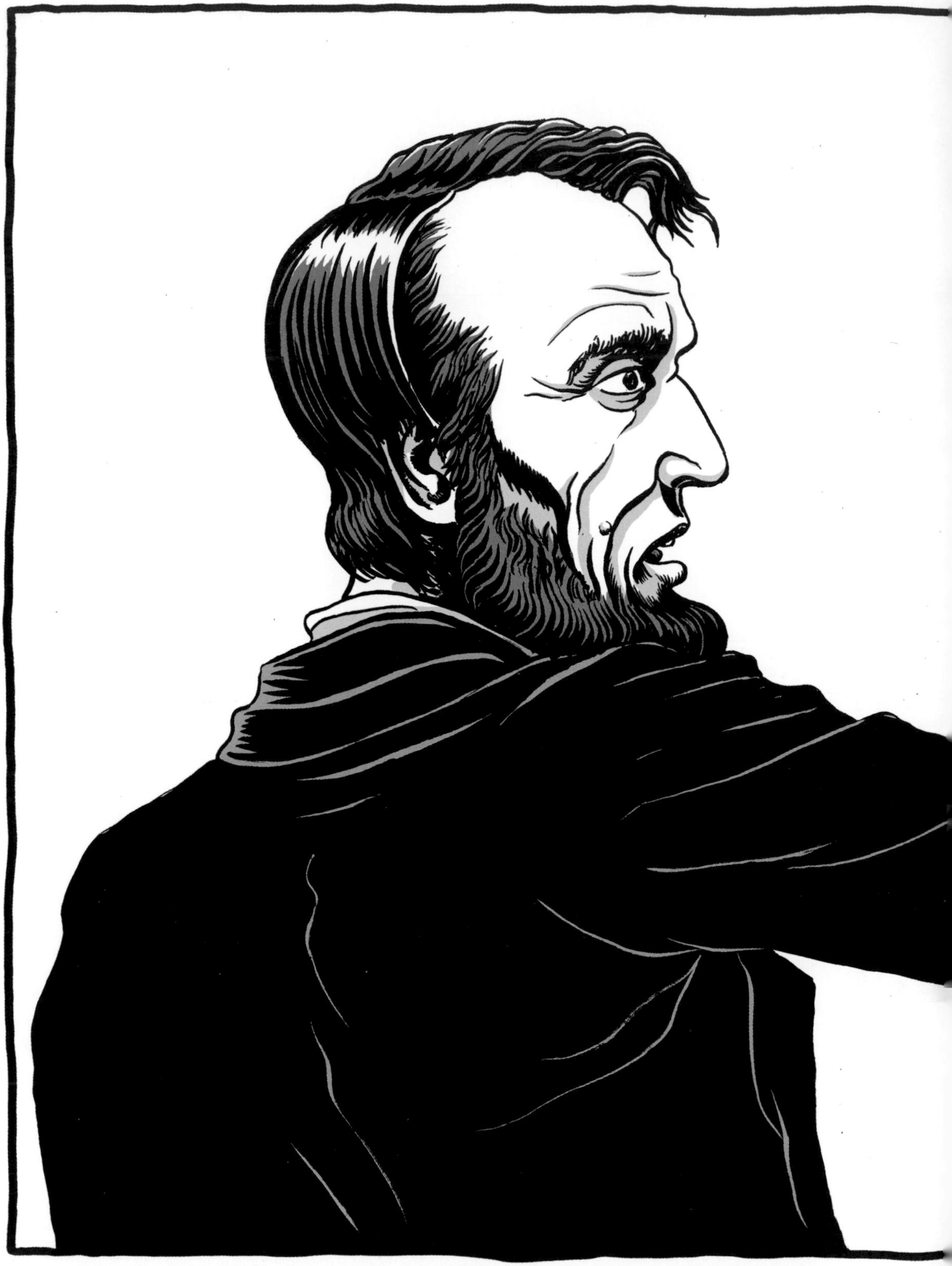

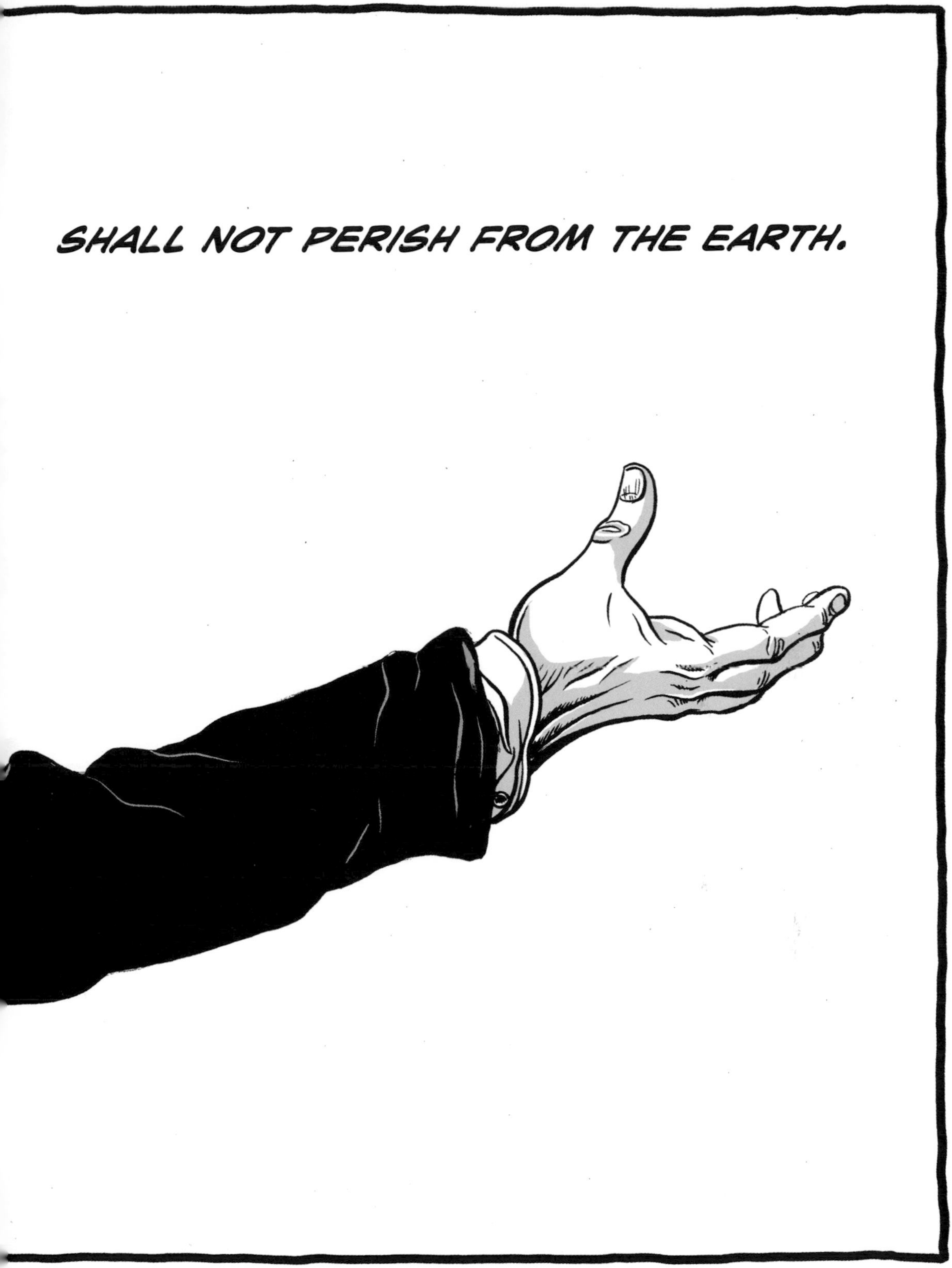
SHALL NOT PERISH FROM THE EARTH.

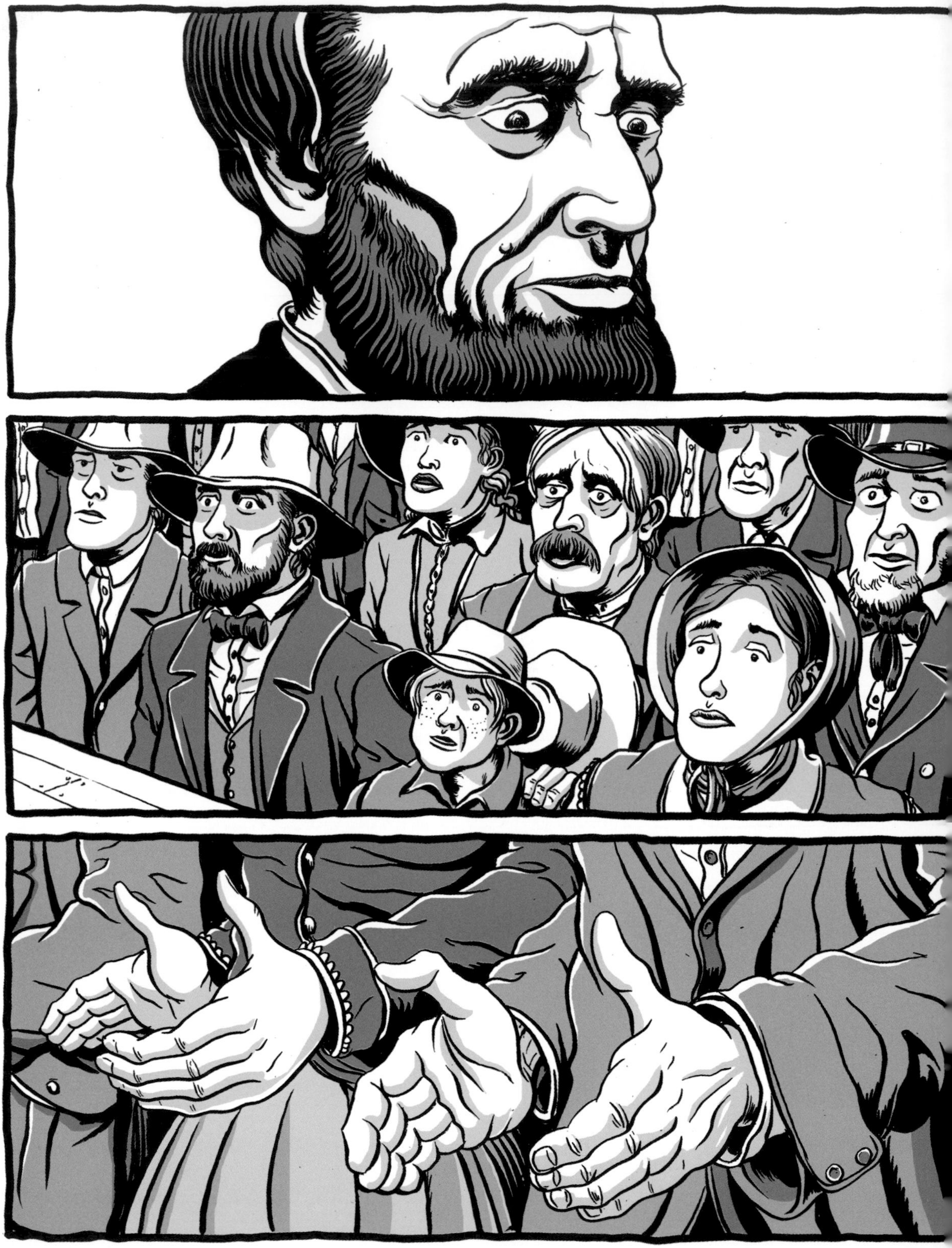

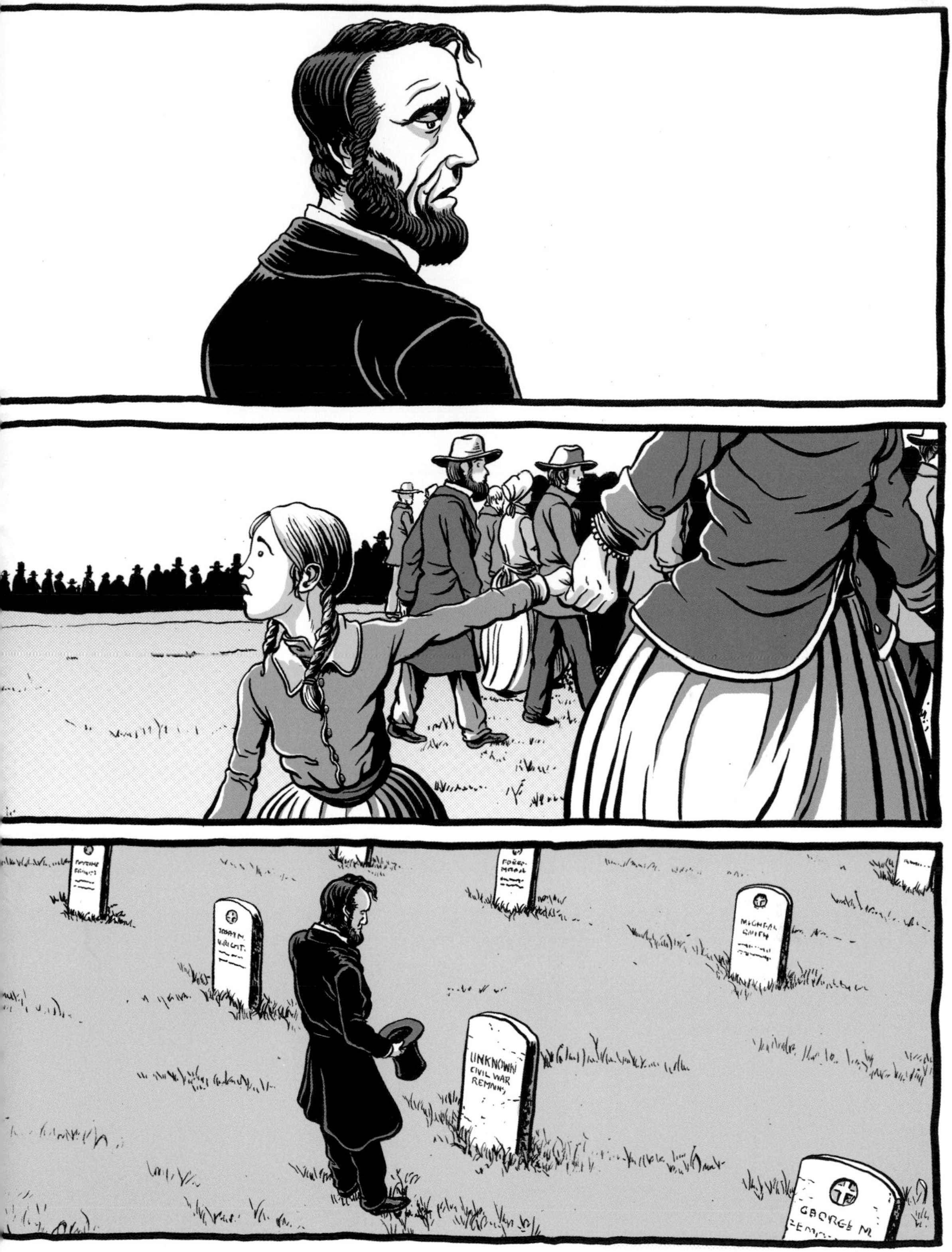
UNKNOWN
CIVIL WAR
REMAINS
GEORGE M.

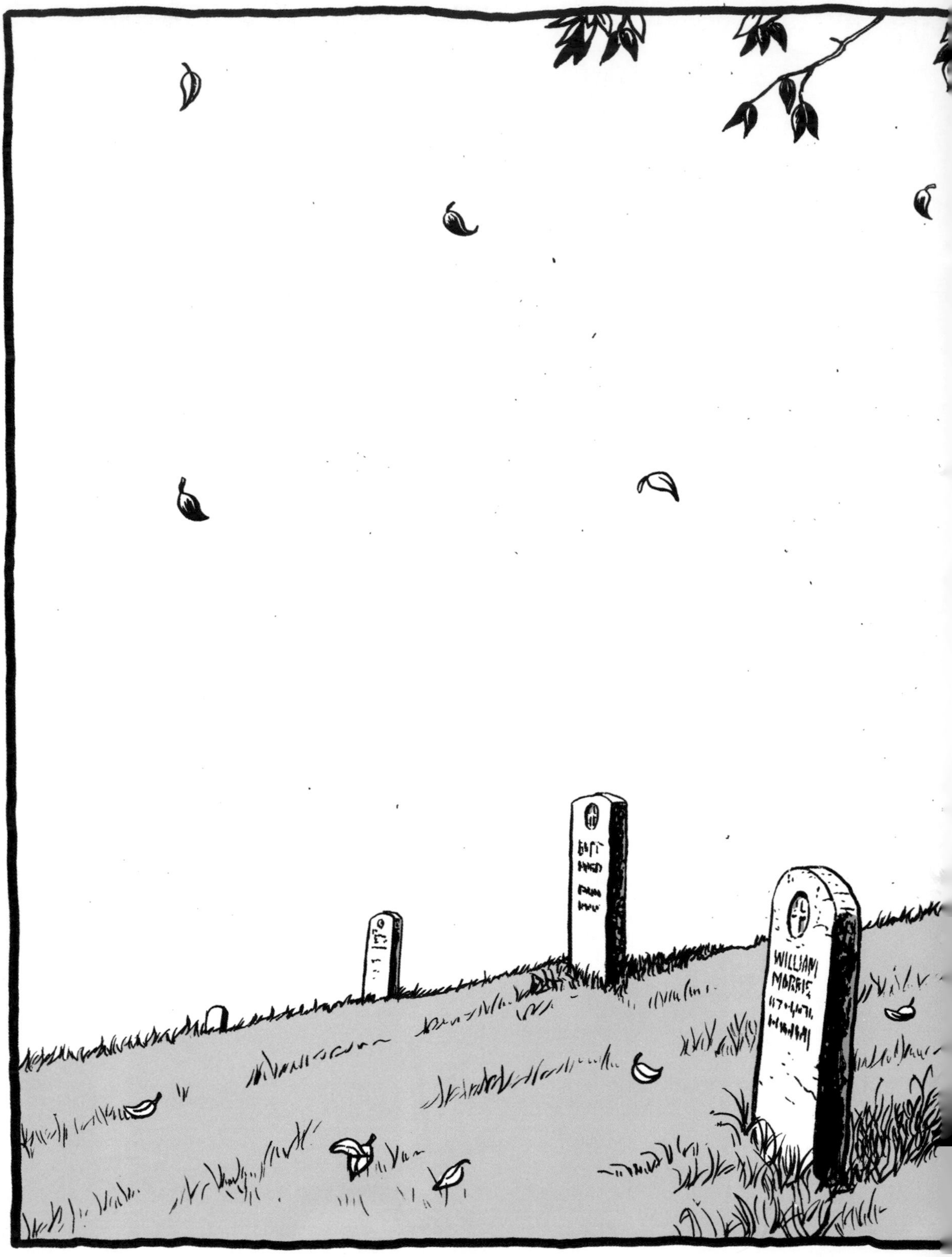
WILLIAM
MORRIS

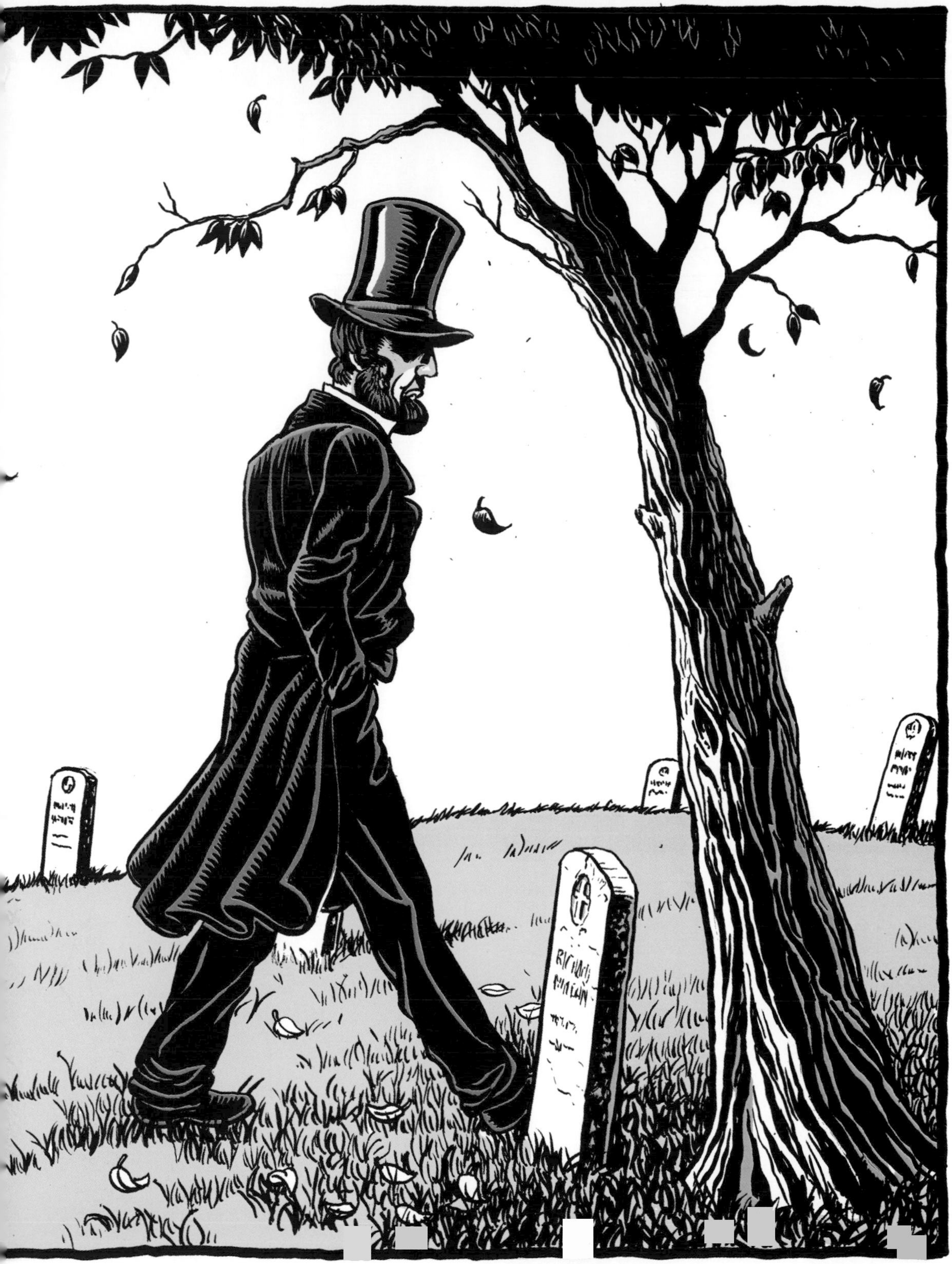

AUTHOR'S NOTES

PAGE 10:

The opening page is a depiction of the Union cavalry riding into the small town of Gettysburg. The region's few freemen (freed African Americans) are leaving the town in anticipation of a Confederate invasion. During the Civil War, runaway slaves and free African Americans captured by the Confederates were treated harshly; they were frequently marched back to the South and forced into slave labor.

PAGE 11:

Union brigadier general John Buford (1826–1863) arrived in Gettysburg on June 30, 1863. He realized the Confederate army was about to launch a major invasion of the Northern states. He was ordered by Lincoln "to hold Gettysburg at all costs." He is considered one of the Union's heroes at Gettysburg for holding off the much larger Confederate forces until Northern reinforcements arrived. The conversation he has with the subordinate was taken from contemporary recorded dialogue.[1]

PAGES 12–16:

These pages cover the events on July 1, 1863, the first day of the battle of Gettysburg. Brigadier General John Buford made a tactical decision to retreat and delay the battle so that the incoming Union reinforcements could secure Cemetery Ridge just south of the town. This retreat—into the advancing Confederate army—led to the capture and death of thousands of Union soldiers. However, the delay also ensured that the Union would have the strategic advantage of high ground for its own defense in the battle.

Confederate general Robert E. Lee (1807–1870) made an overconfident decision to allow the Northern army to choose the theater of battle; it is considered one of his greatest military follies. As evening fell on Gettysburg, both sides were positioning their massive armies in preparation for what they both knew would be a terrible clash the next day.

In the last three panels of page 16, Confederate generals Robert E. Lee and James Longstreet (1821–1904) make plans for the next day's battle. The conversation the two men have about the Union position is taken from dialogue recorded at the time.[2]

PAGES 17–19:

These pages cover the events on the small, tree-covered mountain called Little Round Top and the exploits of the 20th Maine Volunteer Infantry Regiment led by Colonel Joshua L. Chamberlain (1828–1914). Little Round Top is considered one of the most famous battles of the entire Civil War. The pages are based on the account (excerpted here) that Chamberlain recorded of the battle:

The roar of all this tumult reached us on the left and heightened the intensity of our resolve. . . . The crush of musketry gave way to cuts and thrusts, grapplings and wrestlings. The edge of conflict swayed to and fro, with wild pools and eddies. At times I saw around me more of the enemy than of my own men; gaps opening, swallowing, closing again with sharp, convulsive energy; squads of stalwart men who had cut their way through us,

disappearing as if translated all around me, strange, mingled roar-shouts of defiance, rally and desperation; and underneath, murmered [sic] entreaty and stifled moans; gasping prayers, snatches of Sabbath song, whispers of loved names; everywhere men torn and broken, staggering, creeping, quivering on the earth, and dead faces with strangley [sic] fixed eyes staring stark into the sky.[3]

On page 18, in the middle right panel, I've drawn a window that has been cracked by a bullet. Although this particular incident did not happen at Little Round Top, it symbolizes the only recorded civilian death at Gettysburg. This is a small reference to Ginnie Wade, twenty years old, who was baking bread when a stray bullet struck and killed her.[4]

PAGES 20–23:

July 3, 1865, was the third and last day of the conflict. These pages illustrate the infamous blunder of Pickett's charge. General Lee wanted to break the Union line in the middle and ordered General Longstreet to direct a massive attack on the position. In the early afternoon the Southern army fired more than 150 cannons on the Union line, the largest artillery barrage of the entire war.

The Union knew that an infantry charge would follow the bombardment and withheld its 80 cannons in anticipation of the assault. When the Confederate cannons stopped, General George Pickett (1825–1875) made his charge. He ordered some 12,000 Confederates to march across an open field, almost a mile long, straight toward the Union army. As soon as the Confederate soldiers stepped onto the field, the Union cannons began to fire into their vast ranks.

More than half the Confederate attackers never returned from the charge. As they retreated from the Union line, General Lee tried to rally the soldiers into defensive positions to stave off a counterattack. When he called upon Pickett to assemble his division, the devastated Pickett replied, "General Lee, I have no division now."[5] General Lee finally realized the scope of his mistake. Replying to heavy criticism from his staff, Lee remarked that day, "Never mind, General. All this has been my fault. It is I who have lost this fight, and you must help me out the best way you can."[6]

PAGES 24–25:

These pages illustrate my interpretation of the writings of Confederate general John Imboden (1823–1895), who arrived at Gettysburg too late to participate in the battle. Imboden was ordered by Lee to wait for him at his headquarters:

When he arrived there was not even a sentinel on duty at his tent, and no one of his staff was awake. The moon was high in the clear sky and the silent scene was unusually vivid. As he approached and saw us lying on the grass under a tree, he spoke, reined in his jaded horse, and essayed to dismount. The effort to do so betrayed so much physical exhaustion that I hurriedly rose and stepped forward to assist him, but before I reached his side he had succeeded in alighting, and threw his arm across the saddle to rest, and fixing his eyes upon the ground leaned in silence and almost motionless upon his equally weary horse,—the two forming a striking and never-to-be-forgotten group. . . . I ventured to remark, in a sympathetic tone, and in allusion to his great fatigue:

He looked up, and replied mournfully: "Yes, it has been a sad, sad day to us," and immediately relapsed into his thoughtful mood and attitude. Being unwilling again to intrude upon his reflections, I said no more. After perhaps a minute or two, he suddenly straightened up to his full height, and turning to me with more animation

and excitement of manner than I
had ever seen in him before, for he
was a man of wonderful equanimity,
he said in a voice tremulous with
emotion: "I never saw troops behave
more magnificently than Picket's [sic]
division of Virginians did today in
that grand charge upon the enemy. And
if they had been supported as they were
to have been—but, for some reason
not yet fully explained to me, were
not—we would have held the position
and the day would have been ours."
After a moment's pause he added in a
loud voice, in a tone almost of agony,
"Too bad! Too bad! OH! TOO BAD!"[7]

The battle was over and the South had lost.
The next day Lee commanded the Confederate
army to begin the retreat back to the South.

PAGES 28–29:

July 4, 1863. Now it was
possible to start to make
an account of the
terrible cost of this war.
The Union army pursued Lee's defeated
Confederates out of Gettysburg, leaving
behind the dead and wounded. Thousands of
wounded stumbled into the small town from
the battlefield, seeking whatever assistance
they could find. The sheer number of

casualties pouring in from every direction
soon overwhelmed Gettysburg.

The total number of casualties for both
sides has been estimated at more than
40,000. There were almost 8,000 dead lying
on the battlefields and in hastily constructed
field hospitals. Nearly 30,000 wounded
wandered in and around the beleaguered
town, seeking medical aid. More than 11,000
were reported missing or captured. All told,
the number of casualties outnumbered the
small city's population nearly twenty to one.

PAGES 30–31:

These pages depict the
military and civilian
hospitals and the horrors
that took place in them
in the days that followed the battle. The text
is taken from volunteer nurses Eliza Farnham
and Emily Souder of Gettysburg. I've
combined these two women into one
figurative representation as she strolls
through the streets and field hospitals.

As the panels follow the nurse, we see
the astonishing transformation that
Gettysburg underwent, from a quiet rural
city to one vast hospital and morgue. The
Union army left only a handful of doctors
to treat the injured, far too few to make
any difference. But, as news quickly spread
across the Northern states by telegraph and

newspapers, thousands of volunteers from churches and charitable organizations came to help.

In panel three of page 30, there is a mass of rotting horse carcasses. It has been estimated that more than 3,000 horses were killed during the campaign. Combine that with the thousands of dead soldiers left unburied on the battlefields and the hot July summer sun, and the putrid stench that enveloped the city can easily be imagined. The urgent need to treat so many wounded had left these corpses exposed, some for weeks, before they could be hastily buried or burned.

On page 31 I show a brief glimpse of Civil War–era medicine. There were many advances in surgery and pharmaceuticals during this time, but they were often not applied. Civil War surgeons used modern sedatives like morphine to treat a patient's pain but then would attend to the injury with dirty tools and hands, even though disinfectants were available and the understanding of their usefulness was rising. Often the disinfectant was used too late to do any good.

Dysentery, an intestinal infection, killed more soldiers on both sides than bullets or cannons. Of the 620,000 who died during the war, it is estimated that more than 400,000 succumbed to disease.

PAGES 32–35: On these pages we follow the Civil War photographer Timothy O'Sullivan (1840–1882) as he documents with his camera the terrible cost of the battle. O'Sullivan at the time was working for the photo studio of Alexander Gardner (1821–1882). Gardner later produced a book called *Gardner's Photographic Sketch Book of the War*, where O'Sullivan's, Gardner's, and others' photos were printed along with text about the war. The text and photos rendered on these pages are based on that book.

List of reproduced photos on page 33:
Panel 1: "Body of Confederate sharpshooter, Gettysburg, Pennsylvania" (1863; O'Sullivan)
Panel 2: "Field Where General Reynolds Fell, Gettysburg" (1863; O'Sullivan)
Panel 3: "Confederate dead, view looking toward the orchard on the Rose farm" (1863; O'Sullivan)
Panel 4: "Incidents of War Gettysburg" (1863; O'Sullivan)

Here is more of the text from Gardner's book:

Slowly, over the misty fields of Gettysburg—as all reluctant to expose their ghastly horrors to the light—came the sunless morn, after the retreat by Lee's broken army. Through the shadowy vapors, it was, indeed, a "harvest of death" that was presented; hundreds and hundreds of torn Union and rebel soldiers—although many of the former were already interred— strewed the now quiet fighting ground, soaked by the rain, which for two days had drenched the country with its fitful showers.

A battle has often been the subject of elaborate description, but it can perhaps best be described in one simple word—devilish. . . .

Such a picture conveys a useful moral: It shows the blank horror and reality of war, in opposition to its pageantry. Here are the dreadful details! Let them aid in preventing such another calamity falling upon the nation.[8]

PAGES 36–37: Pictured in these pages is the arrival of Pennsylvania governor Andrew Curtin (1817–1894) in the town of Gettysburg, after he had viewed the battlefields. He came to Gettysburg to discuss the building of a

memorial with David Wills (1831–1894) and David McConaughy (1823–1902). This text is, for the most part, fictional, loosely based on what the men said and the actions they took.[9]

Attorney McConaughy was the man who first proposed the construction of a national cemetery at Gettysburg. After the battle he began to acquire the land and organize the construction of what would become the national cemetery. He worked—and sometimes argued with—David Wills, who managed everything, from selecting architect William Saunders to arranging the speakers and dignitaries who would attend the ceremony. The letter that Lincoln holds on page 37 is the invitation penned by Wills.

PAGES 38–39: These pages depict the construction of the Gettysburg Memorial and the exhuming and transferring of the thousands of dead to be buried there. The dialogue between David Wills and William Saunders is pieced together from letters and documents from the time.[10]

The construction of the Soldiers National Cemetery and memorial happened at a mind-boggling pace. The battle had taken place in

July of 1863 and the dedication service was in November. William Saunders arrived in Gettysburg in September and completed the memorial in the two short months before the dedication. Pictured in the first panel of page 38 is the construction of the gatehouse.

The exhuming and reburying of the dead was the most monumental task Saunders and Wills had to face. It was directed by a local African-American freeman, Basil Biggs (1819–1906). Thousands of bodies had to be painstakingly identified, transferred, and reburied according to unit and state. More than 3,000 soldiers' remains were found and placed within the cemetery.

PAGES 40–41:

These pages detail Lincoln's travels from Washington to Gettysburg by rail. The train was pulling specially designed executive cars. (There were four cars, but in order to feature Lincoln's car, I have depicted only one.) The cars were of the highest standard of luxury of the day. Lincoln's car was considered a marvel. It had a sitting room, a bedroom, and a balcony off the back.

In the second panel on page 40, Lincoln is contemplating a piece of writing. The actual time of the composition of the address is not known and it is popular myth that he wrote it on the train. The African-American man sitting with Lincoln is William H. Johnson (dates unknown), Lincoln's personal valet and friend, and probably the only African American who rode in the train or attended the ceremony in a formal capacity. The crowds in the third panel are cheering Lincoln at Camden Station in Baltimore, where the train made a brief stop before pushing onward toward Gettysburg.

PAGES 42–43:

These pages cover the late afternoon and evening of Lincoln's arrival in Gettysburg. Lincoln's arrival has been long awaited in Gettysburg, and the crowds of people from all over the region are exuberant. Some accounts put the number at 50,000 in attendance at the memorial service, though most agree it was roughly 20,000. [11]

Lincoln freely made his way through the crowds, protected only by bodyguard Ward Hill Lamon (1828–1893) and valet William H. Johnson. The president finally entered the house of David Wills, where he stayed the night. Lincoln was most likely in a somber mood. He was reluctant to leave Washington, where Thomas Lincoln, one of his children, was severely ill. Throughout that night, Lincoln received telegrams from Mary Todd Lincoln concerning his son's condition.

On page 43 the large crowd outside the Wills house serenades the president with a rendition of "John Brown's Body." The song celebrates the abolitionist hero who was hanged after attempting to inspire a slave revolt at Harpers Ferry, in what was then Virginia, in 1859. The song took the country by storm and inspired Julia Ward Howe to write "The Battle Hymn of the Republic" in 1861.

PAGES 44–47:
These pages chronicle Lincoln's arrival at the memorial and the speech given by Edward Everett. Although the Gettysburg Address is considered to be one of the greatest American political speeches, Everett's speech was actually the main event of the day. Everett was known as the greatest orator of his time. Edward Everett spoke for nearly two hours that day. The speech he delivered was considered one of his finest and was reproduced in newspapers across the nation.

PAGES 48–65:
Within these pages I attempted to illustrate the solemn and timeless words of Abraham Lincoln's most famous speech, the Gettysburg Address. Some of the images are quite literal and others a metaphorical interpretation. The following paragraphs will explain some of the imagery and individuals I chose to bring the speech to life.

PAGES 48–49:
It was a fine November day, and many thousands of people had crammed themselves within earshot to hear the orations. Lincoln knew he was not the star of the day; that was Everett. Lincoln was giving the closing remarks at an immensely sad funeral.

PAGE 50:
Depicted in panel two are some of the Founding Fathers of the nation: (left to right) John Adams, John Hancock, Thomas Jefferson.

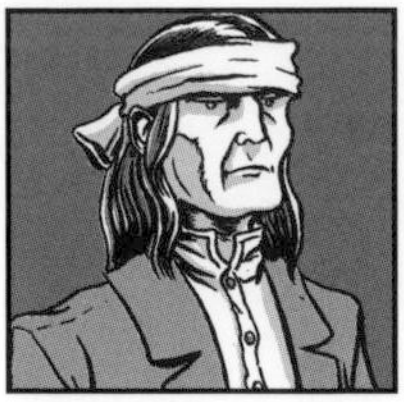

PAGE 51: The last panel on this page loosely depicts the general ethnic groups that made up the population of the United States in the 1860s—blacks, whites, Asians, and Native Americans.

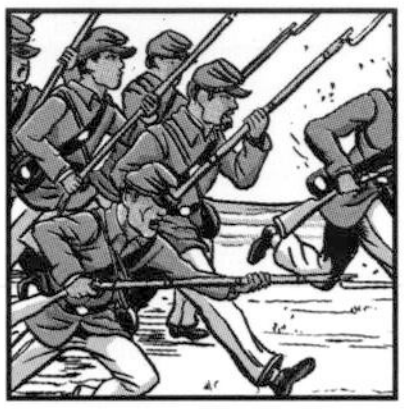

PAGE 52: The Union soldiers pictured here are of the 54th Massachusetts Volunteer Infantry, the regiment that led the charge on Fort Wagner, South Carolina, in 1863.

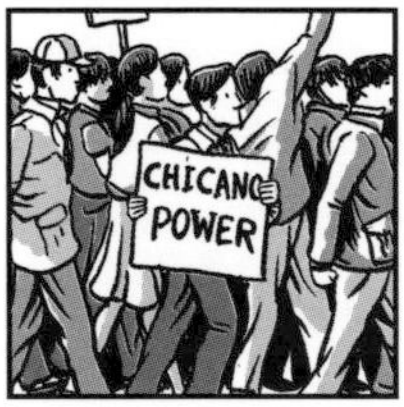
CHICANO
POWER

PAGES 58–59: These pages depict a literal march through the history of civil rights movements: abolitionists and the Union army; women's suffragists; the labor movement; the civil rights movement; the American Indian movement; the Chicano movement; the United Farm Workers movement; the gay rights movement.

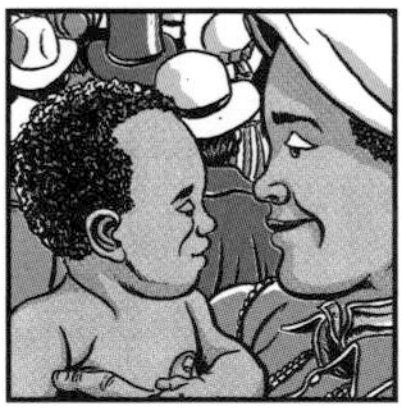

PAGE 62: Although there is no documentation that any African Americans (other than William H. Johnson) were present at the Gettysburg Address, there were more than 180 African Americans living in or near Gettysburg at the time. Gettysburg was also one of the many "stations" of the Underground Railroad, owing to its proximity to the Mason-Dixon line. Basil Biggs, the African-American contractor who managed the reburial of the soldiers at the national cemetery, often used his property to escort runaway slaves to the next stop on the railroad.

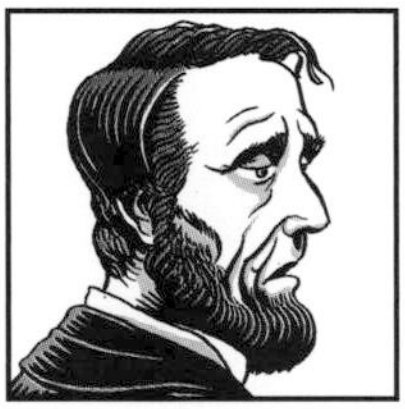

PAGES 66–67: There were no cheers at the end of Lincoln's speech. It was a funeral, a solemn event, and he was not the main orator. In fact, Lincoln himself didn't think much of the speech. He felt certain that his Emancipation Proclamation would be the only prose he would be remembered for.

THE GETTYSBURG ADDRESS

FOUR SCORE AND SEVEN YEARS AGO our fathers brought forth on this continent, a new nation, conceived in liberty, and dedicated to the proposition that all men are created equal.

Now we are engaged in a great civil war, testing whether that nation, or any nation so conceived and so dedicated, can long endure. We are met on a great battle-field of that war. We have come to dedicate a portion of that field, as a final resting place for those who here gave their lives that that nation might live. It is altogether fitting and proper that we should do this.

But, in a larger sense, we can not dedicate—we can not consecrate—we can not hallow—this ground. The brave men, living and dead, who struggled here, have consecrated it, far above our poor power to add or detract. The world will little note, nor long remember what we say here, but it can never forget what they did here. It is for us the living, rather, to be dedicated here to the unfinished work which they who fought here have thus far so nobly advanced. It is rather for us to be here dedicated to the great task remaining before us—that from these honored dead we take increased devotion to that cause for which they gave the last full measure of devotion—that we here highly resolve that these dead shall not have died in vain—that this nation, under God, shall have a new birth of freedom—and that government of the people, by the people, for the people, shall not perish from the earth.

BIBLIOGRAPHY

Bates, Samuel P. *Martial Deeds of Pennsylvania.* Philadelphia: T. H. Davis & Co., 1875.

Boritt, Gabor. *The Gettysburg Gospel.* New York: Simon & Schuster, 2006.

Eckenrode, Hamilton James, and Bryan Conrad. *James Longstreet: Lee's War Horse.* Chapel Hill: University of North Carolina Press, 1986.

Gardner, Alexander. *Gardner's Photographic Sketch Book of the War.* Washington, D.C.: Philp & Solomons, 1865–66.

McPherson, James. *Hallowed Ground: A Walk at Gettysburg.* New York: Crown Publishing, 2003.

Persico, Joseph E. *My Enemy, My Brother: Men and Days of Gettysburg.* New York: Da Capo Press, 1996.

Reid, Ronald F. *Edward Everett: Unionist Orator.* New York: Greenwood Press, 1990.

Renehan, Edward J., Jr. *The Secret Six.* Columbia: University of South Carolina Press, 1996.

Reynolds, David S. *John Brown, Abolitionist.* New York: Knopf, 2005.

Wheeler, Richard J. *Witness to Gettysburg.* Mechanicsburg, PA: Stackpole Books, 2006.

ENDNOTES

1. Wheeler, *Witness to Gettysburg.*
2. Eckenrode, *James Longstreet.*
3. www.nps.gov/archive/gett/getttour/sidebar/chambln.htm
4. www.jennie-wade-house.com/jennie-wade-monument.htm
5. Persico, *My Enemy, My Brother.*
6. McPherson, *Hallowed Ground.*
7. www.eyewitnesstohistory.com/gtburg2.htm
8. Gardner, *Gardner's Photographic Sketch Book.*
9. Wheeler, *Witness to Gettysburg.*
10. Bates, *Martial Deeds of Pennsylvania.*
11. www.eyewitnesstohistory.com/gtsburgaddress.htm

WEBLIOGRAPHY

http://rmc.library.cornell.edu/7milVol/index.html

http://rmc.library.cornell.edu/gettysburg

www.brotherswar.com/Gettysburg_Day_1.htm

www.eyewitnesstohistory.com/cwfrm.htm

www.loc.gov/index.html

www.jennie-wade-house.com

www.nps.gov/gett